COOKING WITH
Bon Appétit

COOKING WITH
Bon Appétit

Easy Entrées

THE KNAPP PRESS
Publishers
Los Angeles

Copyright © 1987 by Knapp Communications Corporation

Published by The Knapp Press
5900 Wilshire Boulevard, Los Angeles, California 90036

Library of Congress Cataloging in Publication Data

Main entry under title:

Easy entrées.

(Cooking with Bon appétit)
Includes index.
1. Cookery (Entrées) I. Series.
TX740.E27   1987   641.8′2   87-3738
ISBN 0-89535-183-8

On the cover: *One-hour Mixed Grill Couscous. Photo by Dicke Sharpe.*

Printed and bound in the United States of America

10   9   8   7   6   5   4   3   2   1

Contents

Foreword vii

1 Soups, Salads and Sandwiches 1
    Soups   2
    Salads   7
    Sandwiches   15

2 Pasta, Vegetables, Eggs
and Cheese 19
    Pasta   20
    Vegetables   25
    Eggs   29
    Cheese   35

3 Meat 41
    Beef   42
    Veal   57
    Lamb   59
    Pork   65

4 Poultry 75

5 Seafood 93
    Fish   94
    Shellfish   104

Index 115

🍃 Foreword

In our often hectic, fast-paced world, the idea of food that is easy to prepare yet delicious and satisfying is certainly an appealing one. This cookbook provides some delicious possibilities for main courses that are quick to make, imaginative and great tasting.

These entrées work beautifully for every day of the week and practically every occasion: On a busy weeknight, when the nicest thing you can do for yourself and your family is to prepare a nutritious stew or healthful seafood salad. Or for entertaining any night of the week, whether it's a casual, last-minute supper or an elegant, plan-ahead dinner.

And not to be overlooked are those precious weekends when, chances are, you don't want to spend all day cooking in the kitchen. Our selections include everything from quiche and chili for an informal meal, to elegant grilled meats and seafood with innovative sauces and accompaniments. Brunches, suppers and family dinners can be easy and fun, with such entrée suggestions as our many superb egg dishes, sandwiches and soups.

Many of the recipes in this book have built-in tips for ease in cooking and menu planning. But here's an additional hint from the experts: Plan ahead. It's much easier to make a good last-minute dish if you keep your pantry well stocked with a variety of vinegars and oils, beef and chicken stock, dried mushrooms, pasta and rice, herbs and spices and other flavorful essentials. Whenever you can, make extra and freeze portions of stock, soups, stews and other foods that can be defrosted and reheated for a homemade meal.

Some of our recipes call for cooking in the microwave; and having a food processor to chop, slice and mix ingredients is often a time-saving bonus. But you don't really need any special equipment to make these delicious entrées— just good-quality ingredients and friends and family ready to enjoy wholesome food that is simply and thoughtfully prepared.

1 ❦ Soups, Salads and Sandwiches

Soups are generally not what come to mind when you think of quick or easy food. The need for long, slow simmering tends to keep most of us from attempting a main-dish soup unless we have all day to spend cooking. But take a look at the easy recipes in this chapter: thick vegetable-based soups like Hearty Beef and Vegetable (page 4), creamy chowders like New England-style Clam (page 7), a rich French country Soupe de Poissons (page 6) and a hearty Kielbasa-Split Pea Soup (page 5). To make preparation even easier, use the food processor to chop up vegetables and herbs. And if you don't have a good homemade soup stock on hand in the freezer, substitute a good-quality unsalted canned variety.

What could be more simple, more refreshing, on a warm spring afternoon than a colorful main-dish salad filled with garden-fresh vegetables and herbs, meat or seafood and tossed with a cool vinaigrette or creamy herbed dressing? Our selection of recipes includes delicious variations on classic salads, such as Chicken Salad with Pesto Dressing (page 8) and a low-calorie Tuna and Green Bean Salad with Yogurt-Dill Dressing (page 11). For a change of pace, try the unusual Scotch Salmon Salad with Creamy Lime Dressing (page 12) or Curried Beef and Pasta Salad with Chutney Dressing (page 14). Served with a light soup, crunchy homemade breadsticks and fresh fruit and cheese, these salads make satisfying meal.

Sandwiches—the original meal-to-go—are quick, easy and popular. Why not lift them from brown-bag status to the dinner table? Here you'll find Bourbon Beef Sandwiches (page 16), served on French rolls and doused with a rich sauce; Open-face Quesadillas (page 16), spicy cheese, bell peppers and avocado, topped with a zesty salsa; and Rio Grande Fajitas (page 18), a colorful do-it-yourself dish for your next barbecue.

 Soups

Autumn Soup

This soup, which includes a bountiful array of autumn vegetables, takes its inspiration from the soups of Italy.

10 to 12 servings

¼	cup olive oil
2	onions, chopped
3	leeks (white part only), cleaned and thinly sliced
2	garlic cloves, minced
4	celery stalks, chopped
2	small turnips, peeled and chopped
2	carrots, peeled and chopped
2	parsnips, peeled and chopped
1	red bell pepper,* seeded and chopped
1	green bell pepper, seeded and chopped
8	cups rich chicken stock
4	cups cooked small white beans
1	tablespoon chopped fresh basil or 1 teaspoon dried, crumbled

1	2-inch fresh rosemary sprig or large pinch of dried, crumbled
1	bay leaf
	Juice of ½ lemon
2	tablespoons olive oil
1	pound mild Italian sausage
2	cups shredded savoy or other green cabbage (½ small head)
1	cup shredded fresh spinach leaves (½ bunch)
	Salt and freshly ground pepper
¼	cup minced fresh parsley
	Freshly grated Parmesan cheese
	Sauce Verte**

Heat ¼ cup olive oil in large saucepan or Dutch oven over medium heat. Add onion, leek and garlic and cook, stirring frequently, until onion is soft and translucent, about 8 minutes. Add celery, turnip, carrot, parsnip and bell peppers and toss to coat with oil. Stir in stock, beans, basil, rosemary, bay leaf and lemon juice and bring to simmer. Reduce heat to medium-low and simmer 10 minutes. Discard rosemary sprig and bay leaf. *(Soup can be prepared up to 2 days ahead to this point and refrigerated.)*

Heat 2 tablespoons olive oil in large skillet over medium-high heat. Add sausage and sauté until cooked through. Drain on paper towels. Cut into ½-inch-thick slices.

About 10 minutes before serving, bring soup to simmer. Add sausage and cabbage and simmer until cabbage is tender. Add spinach and simmer until wilted, about 3 minutes. Season soup with salt and pepper. Stir in parsley. Ladle into heated bowls. Serve with grated Parmesan and Sauce Verte.

*If unavailable, use 2 green peppers total.

**Sauce Verte

Stir a spoonful or two of this into the soup for more flavor.

Makes about ⅔ cup

½	cup crumbled stale French or Italian bread
1	tablespoon red wine vinegar
½	cup chopped fresh parsley
1	hard-cooked egg, coarsely chopped
2	cornichons or tiny dill pickles, chopped

1	tablespoon chopped capers
1	anchovy fillet, chopped
1	garlic clove, halved
2	tablespoons olive oil
¼	teaspoon fresh lemon juice

Place bread in processor or blender and sprinkle with vinegar. Add parsley, egg, pickles, capers, anchovy and garlic and mix until finely minced. With machine running, slowly add olive oil and lemon juice and blend thoroughly (sauce will be thick).

Sauce can be prepared up to 2 days ahead, covered and refrigerated. Bring to room temperature before serving.

Minestrone with Winter Pesto Sauce

A light vegetable puree thickens the broth to make it rich and nutritious. A dollop of pesto sets the soup off perfectly.

Makes about 12 cups

½ cup dried navy beans, rinsed and sorted

4 large garlic cloves
4 medium onions, quartered
3 medium celery stalks, peeled and cut into 1-inch pieces
1 medium potato, peeled and quartered
2 tablespoons olive oil
5½ cups beef stock
2 medium tomatoes, peeled, seeded and quartered

6 tablespoons tomato paste
3 medium carrots, cut into 2-inch lengths
8 ounces fresh green beans, cut into 1½-inch lengths
2 small zucchini, cut into feed tube lengths
2 teaspoons salt
Freshly ground pepper
Winter Pesto Sauce*

Place navy beans in bowl and cover with water. Let soak overnight.

Drain beans. Transfer to large saucepan. Cover generously with water and bring to boil over medium-high heat. Reduce heat and simmer 20 minutes. Drain beans well and set aside.

With processor machine running, drop garlic through feed tube and mince finely. Add onions, celery and potato to work bowl and mince. Heat olive oil in 6- to 8-quart saucepan over low heat. Add onion mixture. Set piece of waxed paper directly atop vegetables and cook 15 minutes, stirring occasionally; do not let vegetables brown. Discard waxed paper. Add 1½ cups stock to vegetables. Cover and cook over medium heat until all vegetables are soft, about 30 minutes. Place tomatoes in work bowl and chop coarsely using several on/off turns. Remove from work bowl and set aside.

Strain onion mixture, returning liquid to saucepan. Transfer vegetables to processor and puree 1 minute, stopping to scrape down sides of work bowl. Stir vegetable puree back into saucepan. Add cooked beans, remaining 4 cups stock, chopped tomatoes and tomato paste and blend well.

Insert medium slicer blade. Stand carrots in feed tube and slice using firm pressure. Add to soup. Place saucepan over medium heat and cook 15 minutes. Stack green beans in feed tube horizontally and slice using light pressure. Remove from work bowl and set aside.

Insert french fry disc. Stand zucchini in feed tube and process using medium pressure. Add green beans and salt and pepper to soup and cook over medium heat 5 minutes. Add zucchini and cook just until all vegetables are crisp-tender, about 5 more minutes. Taste and adjust seasoning. Serve with Winter Pesto Sauce.

*Winter Pesto Sauce

Makes 1½ to 1¾ cups

2 large garlic cloves
3 ounces Parmesan cheese (preferably imported), room temperature, cut into 3 pieces
2 cups tightly packed stemmed spinach leaves *or* Italian parsley, rinsed and dried

½ cup pine nuts or walnuts
2 tablespoons dried basil
1 teaspoon salt
1 cup vegetable oil

With processor machine running, drop garlic through feed tube and mince finely. Add cheese and chop using 4 on/off turns, then process until finely minced, about 1 minute. Add spinach, nuts, basil and salt and blend 10 seconds. With machine running, pour oil through feed tube in slow, steady stream and blend well. Transfer to small bowl and serve immediately.

Braised Irish Vegetable Stew

2 servings; can be doubled or tripled

6 pearl onions, X cut in root ends

2 tablespoons (¼ stick) butter
3 carrots, peeled, halved lengthwise and cut into 1½-inch pieces
2 small turnips, peeled, halved and cut into ¼-inch-thick slices
   Freshly ground pepper

1 teaspoon light brown sugar
1 tablespoon Irish whiskey
1 cup beef broth
¼ small cabbage, cut crosswise into ½-inch-thick slices
   Salt
1 tablespoon chopped fresh mint

Cook onions in small pot of boiling water 1 minute. Drain; peel.

Melt butter in heavy large skillet over high heat. Add onions, carrots and turnips. Sprinkle with pepper. Cook until beginning to brown, stirring frequently, about 7 minutes. Remove skillet from heat. Mix in sugar. Cool 2 minutes. Add whiskey; stir in broth. Return skillet to high heat and bring mixture to boil, scraping up any browned bits. Reduce heat, cover and simmer until vegetables are almost tender, about 15 minutes. Add cabbage, cover and cook until just wilted, about 7 minutes. Uncover, increase heat and boil until liquid is syrupy, about 5 minutes. Season with salt and pepper. Mix in mint and serve.

Hearty Beef and Vegetable Soup

The processor helps cut preparation time for this flavorful soup.

Makes about 12 cups

1 cup fresh parsley leaves
2 medium garlic cloves
3 medium onions, quartered
1½ pounds lean beef chuck, cut into 1-inch cubes and refrigerated

1 14½-ounce can whole tomatoes, drained (reserve liquid)

1 large baking potato, peeled and quartered

3 medium carrots, cut into feed tube lengths

4 celery stalks, peeled and cut into feed tube lengths
3 cups tomato juice
3 cups beef stock
½ cup pearl barley
1½ teaspoons salt
1 teaspoon dried marjoram, crumbled
1 teaspoon dried thyme, crumbled
1 bay leaf
   Freshly ground pepper

Mince parsley finely in processor; remove from work bowl and set aside. With machine running, drop garlic through feed tube and mince finely. Add onions and chop coarsely using on/off turns. Transfer mixture to 6-quart saucepan. Place meat in work bowl (in 1 or 2 batches, depending on processor capacity) and chop to medium-coarse texture using 6 to 8 on/off turns, then grind to desired fineness. Add to saucepan. Cook over medium heat until browned, 7 minutes, breaking up meat with fork.

With processor chop tomatoes coarsely using 4 on/off turns. Add to meat mixture with reserved liquid.

Insert french fry disc. Process potato using firm pressure. Leave in work bowl.

Change to medium slicer blade. Stand carrots in feed tube and slice using firm pressure. Stand celery in feed tube and slice using medium pressure. Add vegetables to saucepan with tomato juice, stock, barley, salt, herbs and pepper. Place over medium heat and cook uncovered until vegetables are soft, about 50 to 55 minutes. Discard bay leaf. Stir in reserved minced parsley. Taste and adjust seasoning. Serve soup hot.

Kielbasa-Split Pea Soup

Serve this hearty main-dish soup with rye bread.

Makes about 3½ quarts

2 quarts water
1 pound split peas, rinsed
1½ pounds kielbasa sausage, cut into bite-size chunks
Salt and freshly ground pepper

2 medium boiling potatoes, peeled and cubed
¾ cup diced carrots
½ cup chopped celery

Combine water and peas in heavy large saucepan or Dutch oven. Bring to boil. Add sausage, salt and pepper. Reduce heat, cover and simmer 30 minutes. Add remaining ingredients and continue simmering until soup is slightly thickened and vegetables are tender, about 15 minutes. Serve immediately.

Cream of Chicken Soup with Pimiento

Makes 10 to 11 cups

2 large carrots, cut into feed tube lengths
1 large onion, halved
1 large leek, including 1 inch of green part, cut into feed tube lengths
2 medium celery stalks, peeled and cut into feed tube lengths
8 cups chicken stock
1 3- to 3¼-pound roasting chicken, quartered
2 whole cloves

2 4-ounce jars pimientos, drained
1 cup whipping cream
2 teaspoons Hungarian sweet paprika
½ teaspoon salt or to taste
¼ teaspoon freshly grated nutmeg
Freshly ground pepper

3 tablespoons snipped fresh chives (garnish)

Insert medium slicer blade in processor. Stand carrots and onion in feed tube and slice using firm pressure. Slice leek and celery using medium pressure. Transfer vegetables to 5- to 6-quart saucepan. Add stock, chicken and cloves and bring to simmer over medium-high heat. Reduce heat and simmer 30 minutes. Cool 15 minutes. Discard chicken skin and bones and cut meat into bite-size pieces. Set chicken aside. Discard cloves. *(Can be prepared 1 day ahead to this point, cooled, covered and refrigerated. Cover chicken and refrigerate separately.)* Degrease stock. Cover and simmer until vegetables are very soft, about 30 minutes. Ladle mixture through fine strainer, returning liquid to saucepan.

Insert steel knife in processor. Transfer cooked vegetables to work bowl. Add 1½ jars drained pimientos and puree until smooth, about 1 minute, stopping to scrape down sides of work bowl. Stir puree into liquid in saucepan. Add cream, paprika, salt, nutmeg, pepper and reserved chicken. Adjust seasoning; heat through (do not boil).

Cut remaining pimientos into ⅛-inch julienne. Garnish soup with chives and pimiento julienne and serve.

Soupe de Poissons

8 servings

½ cup olive oil
3 large yellow onions, chopped
1 cup chopped leek
4 garlic cloves, chopped
1½ pounds tomatoes, peeled and chopped
Bouquet garni (2 sprigs celery leaves, 2 sprigs dried fennel or 1 teaspoon fennel seed, 2 to 3 sprigs fresh thyme or 1 teaspoon dried, 1 tablespoon fresh basil or 1 teaspoon dried, 1 bay leaf, ½ teaspoon grated orange peel)

3 to 3½ pounds firm fresh fish, cut into chunks
6 cups boiling water
2 8-ounce bottles clam juice
2 cups dry white wine
Salt and freshly ground pepper

½ teaspoon ground saffron
8 slices dried French bread, rubbed with garlic
½ cup (or more) freshly grated Parmesan cheese
Rouille*

Heat olive oil in large Dutch oven or stockpot over low heat. Add onion, leek and garlic. Top with round of waxed paper or parchment. Cover and cook, stirring occasionally, until vegetables are soft and transparent, about 15 to 20 minutes (do not brown). Increase heat to high. Add tomatoes and bouquet garni. Add fish and cook, stirring constantly, 10 minutes. Add boiling water, clam juice, wine and salt and pepper. Cover partially, reduce heat to medium and cook 25 to 30 minutes.

Strain stock into large bowl, pressing ingredients with back of wooden spoon to extract as much liquid as possible. Discard fish, vegetables and bouquet garni. Bring broth to gentle boil over medium heat. Add saffron and salt and pepper to taste. Ladle into individual bowls. Top each serving with bread slice and sprinkle with about 1 tablespoon Parmesan. Pass Rouille separately.

*Rouille

Makes 1¼ cups

2 small dried red chilies, stemmed
1 small bunch basil leaves (optional)
2 to 3 garlic cloves
Coarse salt and freshly ground pepper
1 thick slice French bread, soaked in water and squeezed dry

1 sweet red bell pepper, broiled, skinned, seeded and ribs removed (optional)
½ to ¾ cup olive oil

Crush dried chilies in large mortar until powdered. Add basil, garlic and salt and pepper and blend to paste. Add bread, sweet pepper and continue blending until pureed. Add ½ cup oil in slow steady stream, stirring constantly with pestle until mixture is consistency of mayonnaise and adding more olive oil as necessary.

Bay Scallop Soup

4 servings

2 8-ounce bottles clam juice
1 tablespoon unsalted butter
½ teaspoon Worcestershire sauce
½ teaspoon dry mustard
⅛ teaspoon garlic powder

⅛ teaspoon celery salt
¾ pound bay scallops
2 egg yolks
1 cup whipping cream
Snipped fresh chives

Combine first 6 ingredients in medium saucepan and bring to boil. Add scallops and simmer gently 3 minutes. Beat yolks with cream in bowl. Ladle about ½ cup hot soup into cream and blend well. Gradually stir cream mixture back into soup. Stir until soup thickens slightly, 1 to 2 minutes. Sprinkle with chives. Serve immediately.

New England-style Clam Chowder

The good-natured contro-versy continues between devotees of New England-style chowder and the Manhattan version. This thick, creamy chowder has not a tomato in sight.

Makes about 8 cups

4 ounces salt pork

3 medium onions, quartered

2 medium celery stalks, cut into 1-inch pieces

2 medium baking potatoes, peeled and cut into thirds

2 10¼-ounce cans whole small clams, drained (reserve liquid) and coarsely chopped

2 cups water

½ teaspoon dried thyme, crumbled

1 bay leaf

½ teaspoon salt
Freshly ground white pepper

2 cups milk

1 cup whipping cream

3 tablespoons unsalted butter

3 tablespoons all purpose flour

Blanch salt pork in boiling water 5 minutes. Drain well; let cool slightly. Cut salt pork into 1-inch cubes.

Combine salt pork, onions and celery in processor work bowl and mince using on/off turns. Transfer to 3-quart saucepan. Bring to simmer over medium heat. Reduce heat to low and cook until vegetables are soft and salt pork is lightly browned, about 15 minutes.

Insert french fry disc in processor. Process potatoes using firm pressure. Remove from work bowl and cut into cubes using sharp knife. Add to onion mixture with clam liquid, water, thyme, bay leaf, salt and pepper. Place over medium heat and cook just until potatoes are crisp-tender, about 12 to 15 minutes. Stir in chopped clams, milk and cream and heat through. Discard bay leaf.

Melt butter in small saucepan over low heat. Stir in flour and cook 1 minute; do not let mixture color. Gradually whisk in 1 cup hot soup liquid. Increase heat to medium and bring to boil, stirring constantly. Return mixture to soup and blend well. Adjust seasoning and serve.

 *Salads*

Chicken and Spinach Salad

6 to 8 servings

3 medium green onions, finely chopped

½ cup olive oil

5 to 6 tablespoons fresh lemon juice

2 to 3 tablespoons chopped fresh dill

2 medium garlic cloves, minced
Salt and freshly ground pepper

2 whole chicken breasts, poached and cut into strips (4 cups)

1 pound fresh spinach, torn into bite-size pieces

3 small zucchini, thinly sliced on diagonal

For dressing: Combine ingredients in small bowl and mix well.

Pour dressing over chicken in shallow dish and marinate in refrigerator overnight. Combine spinach and zucchini in large serving bowl. Add chicken strips with dressing. Toss well and serve.

Napa Cabbage Chicken Salad

2 servings

½ cup fresh orange juice
2 tablespoons sliced carrots
2 tablespoons (¼ stick) butter
1 cup chopped red bell pepper
2 green onions, chopped
¼ medium head Napa cabbage (Chinese cabbage), sliced
2 cups cooked chicken cut into 1½-inch strips
⅓ cup cubed edam cheese
20 seedless green grapes

8 green beans, cut diagonally into 2-inch lengths and parboiled
1 tomato, peeled and sliced
5½ tablespoons rice wine vinegar
¼ cup hazelnut oil
½ teaspoon paprika
½ teaspoon salt
¼ teaspoon dry mustard
⅛ teaspoon cayenne pepper
⅛ teaspoon freshly grated nutmeg
Dash of freshly ground pepper

Heat orange juice in small saucepan over medium-high heat. Add carrots and cook until crisp-tender; drain. Melt butter in small skillet over medium-low heat. Add red pepper and green onions and sauté until beginning to soften, about 5 minutes. Transfer to bowl. Add carrots, sliced cabbage, chicken, cheese, grapes, beans and tomato. Combine remaining ingredients in jar with tight-fitting lid and shake well. Pour over salad and toss to coat.

Chicken Salad with Pesto Dressing

4 to 6 servings

1 tablespoon olive oil
¼ cup pine nuts
1 small garlic clove, finely minced
¼ teaspoon salt

1 cup mayonnaise
1 tablespoon (or more) Spinach Pesto*

2 cups cubed cooked chicken
1 cup spinach julienne
2 tablespoons chopped black olives

Heat oil in heavy small skillet over medium heat. Add nuts, garlic and salt and sauté just until nuts turn golden, being careful not to burn. Cool.

Combine mayonnaise and 1 tablespoon pesto in large bowl. Add chicken, spinach, olives and nuts and toss well. Stir in additional pesto if desired. Serve salad at room temperature.

*Spinach Pesto

This pesto is also delicious tossed with pasta.

Makes about 2 cups

4 medium garlic cloves
1 10-ounce package frozen spinach, thawed and squeezed dry
1 cup chopped fresh parsley
½ cup pine nuts

3 ounces freshly grated Parmesan cheese
2 tablespoons dried basil, crumbled
1 teaspoon salt
1 cup (or more) olive oil

Mince garlic finely in processor. Add spinach, parsley, pine nuts, cheese, basil and salt and process until well blended. With machine running, pour 1 cup oil through feed tube in thin stream. Process just until well mixed, adding more oil if thinner consistency is desired. Cover and refrigerate up to 1 week or freeze up to 3 months. To serve, bring pesto to room temperature and stir well.

Chicken and Vegetable Julienne with Mustard-Walnut Vinaigrette

6 servings

½ cup fresh parsley leaves

Vinaigrette
  ¾ cup safflower oil
  4 tablespoons plus 1½ teaspoons red wine vinegar
4½ teaspoons walnut oil
  1 tablespoon Dijon mustard
  ¾ teaspoon salt
    Freshly ground pepper

  6 small green onions, cut into 2-inch pieces

  5 2-inch-long thick ends of carrots, peeled

  2 medium turnips, peeled and trimmed
  1 teaspoon minced fresh oregano or ¼ teaspoon dried, crumbled

1⅓ pounds skinned, boned and halved chicken breasts (3 whole breasts)
  1 teaspoon Dijon mustard

  2 small heads romaine lettuce, trimmed and sliced
  ½ cup walnut halves, toasted
  2 tablespoons snipped fresh chives

Finely mince parsley in processor. Transfer to small bowl and set aside.

For vinaigrette: In processor blend first 6 ingredients 5 seconds. Set aside.

Change to thin slicer blade. Arrange green onions lengthwise in feed tube and slice using light pressure. Transfer green onions to medium bowl and set aside.

Change to medium slicer blade. Arrange carrots lengthwise in feed tube and slice using firm pressure. Stack slices and arrange lengthwise in feed tube with slices perpendicular to slicing disc. Slice using medium pressure. Set aside. Stand turnips in feed tube and slice using firm pressure. Stack slices and arrange in feed tube with slices perpendicular to slicing disc. Slice using medium pressure. Steam carrots and turnips until crisp-tender, about 2 minutes. Add to sliced green onions. Mix in ⅓ cup vinaigrette, 1 tablespoon minced fresh parsley and oregano.

Pat chicken dry. Heat 3 tablespoons vinaigrette in heavy 10-inch skillet over medium-high heat. Add chicken and cook until meat is opaque and springy to touch, about 3 minutes per side. Transfer to cutting board and cool slightly. Cut across grain into ⅓-inch-thick strips. Return to skillet with ⅓ cup vinaigrette, 2 tablespoons parsley and 1 teaspoon mustard. Toss to coat chicken. (If chicken is pink, cook over low heat until just opaque.) Adjust seasoning. *(Can be prepared 1 day ahead. Wrap chicken, vegetables, parsley and vinaigrette separately and refrigerate. Let stand at room temperature 30 minutes before assembling salad.)*

Toss lettuce with remaining vinaigrette. Divide among plates. Spoon vegetables atop lettuce leaving 2-inch border. Drain chicken and arrange on top. Garnish with walnuts, chives and remaining parsley. Serve immediately.

Chicken Salad Oriental

6 to 8 servings

2 cups peanut oil
10 won ton skins, cut into ½-inch strips
1 head iceberg lettuce, shredded
3 cups shredded cooked chicken
1 cup chopped green onions
2 tablespoons toasted sesame seeds

¼ cup vegetable oil
3 tablespoons rice vinegar
2 tablespoons sugar
1 tablespoon oriental sesame oil
1 teaspoon salt
½ teaspoon freshly ground pepper

Heat peanut oil in heavy large skillet over medium-high heat. Add won ton skins and fry until golden brown, about 1 minute. Remove using slotted spoon and drain on paper towels. Transfer to large bowl. Add lettuce, chicken, onions and sesame seeds. Combine remaining ingredients in jar with tight-fitting lid and shake well. Pour dressing over salad and toss to coat. Serve immediately.

Turkey, Jicama and Bell Pepper Salad

A refreshing summer salad that makes the most of cilantro and mint.

6 servings

1 large garlic clove
1 serrano chili, stemmed
⅔ cup safflower oil
¼ cup red wine vinegar
1 tablespoon dark soy sauce
1 tablespoon fresh lemon juice
1½ teaspoons sugar
1 teaspoon oriental sesame oil
½ teaspoon salt

1 small jicama, peeled and cut to fit feed tube

1 medium red bell pepper
1 medium green bell pepper
1 medium yellow bell pepper

3 large green onions, cut into feed-tube widths
3½ cups cooked turkey or chicken, cut julienne

2 cups fresh cilantro leaves
8 tablespoons fresh mint leaves

4 cups mixed greens (such as green and red leaf lettuce, watercress and Boston lettuce), torn into bite-size pieces
6 fresh cilantro leaves
6 fresh mint leaves

Insert steel knife in processor. With machine running, drop garlic and chili through feed tube and mince. Add safflower oil, vinegar, soy sauce, lemon juice, sugar, sesame oil and salt and blend 3 seconds. Remove dressing from work bowl.

Change to medium slicer blade. Arrange jicama in feed tube and slice using firm pressure. Stack slices and arrange lengthwise in feed tube with slices perpendicular to slicing disc, packing tightly. Slice using medium pressure. Transfer to bowl.

Cut bell peppers lengthwise into 4 pieces each; discard cores and ribs. Stand pepper pieces in feed tube, packing tightly. Slice using light pressure. Add to jicama.

Change to thick slicer blade. Arrange green onions lengthwise in feed tube and slice using light pressure. Add to jicama. Mix in turkey and dressing. Cover and refrigerate 6 hours or overnight.

Using steel knife, finely mince ½ cup cilantro and 2 tablespoons mint.

Just before serving, add minced herbs to turkey salad and toss well. Adjust seasoning. Mix remaining 1½ cups cilantro and 6 tablespoons mint into greens. Divide greens among plates. Mound some of turkey salad in center of each. Garnish with cilantro and mint.

Curried Turkey Salad

4 servings

2 cups cubed cooked turkey or
   chicken
1 large celery stalk, thinly sliced
¼ cup slivered blanched almonds
¼ cup golden raisins
1 medium green onion, thinly sliced
2 tablespoons mango chutney
5 tablespoons Curry Mayonnaise*
   Lettuce
   Mayonnaise

Garnishes
   Hard-cooked eggs (halved)
   Boiled potatoes (halved)
   Cucumber slices
   Fresh pineapple or melon chunks
   Tart apple slices
   Mandarin orange sections
   Steamed carrot chunks
   Steamed green beans
   Steamed broccoli

Combine turkey, celery, almonds, raisins, green onion and chutney in medium bowl. Add 2 tablespoons Curry Mayonnaise and toss to blend. Arrange lettuce on platter. Spoon chicken mixture atop lettuce. Serve with any or all of garnishes. Thin remaining 3 tablespoons Curry Mayonnaise with mayonnaise and serve as dip for garnishes.

*Curry Mayonnaise

Makes 5 tablespoons

3 tablespoons mayonnaise
1 tablespoon curry powder
1 tablespoon Dijon mustard

1 teaspoon fresh lemon juice
1 large garlic clove, minced

Mix all ingredients in small bowl.

Tuna and Green Bean Salad with Yogurt-Dill Dressing

6 servings

Tuna
2 6½-ounce cans solid white tuna in
   water, drained and flaked
3 small celery stalks, finely diced
⅔ cup plain lowfat yogurt
2 tablespoons mayonnaise
2 large shallots, minced
2 tablespoons coarsely chopped
   Italian parsley
2 tablespoons minced fresh dill
   or ½ teaspoon dried dillweed
4 teaspoons well-drained small
   capers
¼ teaspoon grated lemon peel
¼ teaspoon freshly ground pepper

Beans
1 medium red onion, halved
   lengthwise and thinly sliced

1 medium garlic clove, minced
1 medium shallot, minced
⅓ cup minced fresh dill
   or 1½ teaspoons dried dillweed
2 tablespoons minced fresh Italian
   parsley
2 tablespoons olive oil
¼ teaspoon grated lemon peel
2 pounds green beans, trimmed
2 tablespoons chicken broth
   Salt and freshly ground pepper

3 to 4 tablespoons red wine vinegar
   or dill vinegar

For tuna: Combine all ingredients in medium bowl. Cover with plastic wrap and refrigerate overnight.

   For beans: Combine first 7 ingredients in large bowl. Cook beans in large pot of boiling salted water until crisp-tender. Drain well. Place atop onion mixture; do not mix. Cool to room temperature. Add broth, salt and pepper and mix to blend. Cover tightly and refrigerate overnight.

Let tuna and bean mixtures stand at room temperature 45 minutes. Mix 3 tablespoons vinegar into beans. Adjust seasoning. Let stand 10 minutes. Taste and add more vinegar to beans if desired. Mound tuna in center of round platter. Surround with green beans.

Scotch Salmon Salad with Creamy Lime Dressing

6 servings

1 small lime, scored, 1 end cut flat

1 small cucumber, peeled, halved lengthwise, seeded and cut to fit feed tube

4 small green onions, cut into feed-tube widths

2 medium heads Boston lettuce, cored and sliced

Creamy Lime Dressing
¾ cup whipping cream
9 to 10½ teaspoons fresh lime juice

4½ teaspoons minced fresh dill
   or 1 teaspoon dried dillweed
¼ teaspoon salt, or to taste
   Freshly ground white pepper

12 ounces thinly sliced Scotch salmon
1 to 2 tablespoons fresh lime juice
   Snipped fresh dill

Insert medium slicer blade in processor. Stand lime in feed tube and slice using firm pressure. Set aside.

Insert thin slicer blade. Stand cucumber in feed tube and slice using medium pressure. Arrange green onions widthwise in feed tube and slice using light pressure. Transfer to large bowl. Add lettuce and toss to combine.

For dressing: Using steel knife, blend cream, 9 teaspoons lime juice, 4½ teaspoons dill, salt and pepper 3 seconds. Add more lime juice if desired.

Mix dressing into salad. Adjust seasoning. Place salad in center of each plate. Cover with salmon, overlapping slightly. Drizzle with 1 to 2 tablespoons lime juice and sprinkle with white pepper. Arrange lime slice in center of each. Garnish with dill.

Summer Seafood Salade Composée with Tarragon Mayonnaise

Quick to prepare in the processor, the mayonnaise can be used to dress salads all week. The seasoning could also be stirred into 1¼ cups of purchased mayonnaise. If crab is not available, double the amount of shrimp.

2 servings; can be doubled or tripled

6 ounces green beans, trimmed
2 small yellow crookneck squash, ends trimmed
1 small head Boston lettuce
1 large beefsteak tomato, sliced into thick rounds

1 small cucumber, peeled, seeded and cut into ½-inch dice
¼ pound cooked bay shrimp
¼ pound cooked crabmeat
   Tarragon Mayonnaise*

Blanch beans and squash in boiling salted water until beans are just crisp-tender and squash just yields to slight pressure, about 4 minutes. Rinse under cold water; drain thoroughly. Cut squash lengthwise into ⅓-inch-thick strips. Line platter with lettuce. Arrange tomato slices around edge of platter, leaving space between each slice. Combine beans and squash and arrange between tomato slices. Mix cucumber, shrimp, crabmeat and ¼ cup mayonnaise. Mound in center of platter. Serve salad, passing additional mayonnaise separately.

*Tarragon Mayonnaise

Makes about 1½ cups

1 egg, room temperature
2 tablespoons fresh lemon juice
1 tablespoon minced green onion or shallot
2 teaspoons coarse-grained Dijon mustard

½ cup plus 2 tablespoons vegetable oil
½ cup olive oil
1 tablespoon minced fresh tarragon or 1 teaspoon dried, crumbled
Salt and freshly ground pepper

Mix egg, lemon juice, green onion and mustard in processor. With machine running, add both oils through feed tube in slow stream. Mix in tarragon, salt and pepper. *(Can be prepared 5 days ahead, covered and refrigerated.)*

Oriental Shrimp and Vegetable Salad

6 servings

¼ pound snow peas, trimmed

2 large garlic cloves
1 ¾-inch cube fresh ginger, peeled
¼ cup safflower oil
½ teaspoon chili oil*
1¼ pounds uncooked frozen peeled medium to large shrimp (do not thaw)
3 tablespoons rice vinegar*
1 teaspoon oriental sesame oil*
1 teaspoon sugar

1 teaspoon salt
¼ teaspoon five-spice powder*

1 large red bell pepper

1 small jicama, peeled and cut to fit feed tube
6 green onions, including tops, cut into thirds

½ cup cilantro leaves
½ cup dry-roasted cashews

Cook snow peas in boiling salted water until beginning to soften, about 90 seconds. Drain; rinse under cold water. Drain again. Transfer to large bowl.

Insert steel knife in processor. With machine running, drop garlic and ginger through feed tube and mince finely.

Heat both oils in heavy 10-inch skillet over medium-high heat. Add garlic mixture and shrimp in 3 batches and cook until shrimp is just opaque, about 3 minutes. Transfer shrimp to plate using slotted spoon. Add vinegar, sesame oil, sugar, salt and five-spice powder to juices in skillet and bring to boil, scraping up any browned bits. Remove from heat.

Cut bell pepper into 4 pieces, discarding core and seeds.

Insert medium slicer blade in processor. Arrange pepper pieces lengthwise in feed tube, packing tightly. Slice using light pressure. Add pepper slices to snow peas.

Stand jicama in feed tube and slice using firm pressure. Stack slices and arrange lengthwise in feed tube with slices perpendicular to slicing disc, packing tightly. Slice again using medium pressure. Arrange green onions lengthwise in feed tube and slice using light pressure.

Add jicama mixture to snow peas. Add shrimp, pan sauce and cilantro and toss gently to blend. *(Can be prepared 3 days ahead, covered and refrigerated.)* Just before serving, drain any liquid. Mix in cashews. Adjust seasoning.

*Available at oriental markets.

Curried Crab, Garden Pea and Papaya Salad in Papaya Shells

A fresh-tasting, light entrée.

6 servings

3 small firm ripe papayas, halved lengthwise and seeded
1 pound lump crabmeat, picked over and coarsely flaked
1 cup tiny fresh or frozen peas, cooked
2 medium celery stalks, finely diced
¼ cup minced fresh cilantro or snipped fresh dill

Curry Dressing
　Nonstick vegetable oil spray
1 tablespoon unsalted butter
2 medium green onions, minced

1 tablespoon curry powder
¼ teaspoon finely grated lime or lemon peel
　Pinch of dried rosemary, crumbled
　Pinch of ground mace
½ cup plain lowfat yogurt
¼ cup sour cream
3 tablespoons mayonnaise
1½ teaspoons Dijon mustard
¼ teaspoon hot pepper sauce
¼ teaspoon freshly ground pepper

　Thin lime slices
　Fresh cilantro or dill sprigs

Using small knife, cut papaya flesh from skin, leaving ¼-inch-thick shell; leave flesh in place. Cut flesh into ¼-inch dice. Scoop dice onto paper towels. Top with more towels. Drain papaya shells cut side down on paper towels. Combine crab, peas, celery and cilantro or dill in large bowl.

For dressing: Coat heavy small skillet with vegetable spray. Add butter and melt over low heat. Add green onions, curry powder, lime peel, rosemary and mace and stir until onions are tender, about 3 minutes. Transfer mixture to processor or blender. Add all remaining ingredients except lime slices and cilantro. Blend 1½ minutes, stopping once to scrape sides of work bowl.

Add dressing and diced papaya to crab mixture and toss lightly. Cover and refrigerate 3 to 4 hours. Just before serving, toss salad lightly. Mound in papaya shells. Garnish with lime slices and fresh cilantro or dill.

Curried Beef and Pasta Salad with Chutney Dressing

8 servings

1 1½-pound piece sirloin, cooked rare

4 large carrots, peeled and cut into 2½-inch pieces

18 small mushrooms, trimmed, one side cut flat

Chutney Dressing
1 cup safflower oil
½ cup mango chutney

1 egg
2 tablespoons fresh lemon juice
2 tablespoons beef stock
1 tablespoon curry powder, or to taste
¾ teaspoon salt
¼ teaspoon cayenne pepper

8 ounces pasta shells, freshly cooked
1 10-ounce package frozen tiny peas, thawed and drained

Line baking sheet with waxed paper. Cut meat across grain to fit processor feed tube. Set meat on sheet. Freeze until just firm but still easily pierced with tip of sharp knife. *(Can be prepared 1 month ahead. Wrap tightly and return to freezer. Let meat thaw in refrigerator just until easily pierced with knife.)*

Insert medium slicer blade in processor. Arrange carrots lengthwise in feed tube and slice using firm pressure. Stack slices and arrange lengthwise in feed tube with slices perpendicular to slicing disc, packing tightly. Slice using medium pressure. Cook carrots in medium pot of boiling salted water until just tender, about 2 minutes. Drain; rinse under cold water and drain again. Pat dry.

Arrange meat in feed tube to slice across grain. Slice using firm pressure. Stand mushrooms on flat side in feed tube and slice using light pressure. Transfer meat mixture to large bowl. Set aside.

For dressing: Insert steel knife. Blend oil, chutney, egg, lemon juice, stock, curry powder, salt and cayenne until smooth, about 10 seconds.

Add dressing to meat and toss to blend. Mix in carrots, pasta and peas. *(Can be prepared 3 days ahead, covered and refrigerated.)* Adjust seasoning. Let pasta salad stand at room temperature for 20 minutes before serving.

Lentil and Lamb Salad with Curried Apple Vinaigrette

Cooked pork or chicken can be substituted for the lamb in this salad.

4 to 6 servings

1 cup lentils, rinsed and drained

1 cup parsley leaves
1 large Granny Smith apple, cored, peeled and cut into eighths
½ cup safflower oil
¼ cup fresh lemon juice
1 teaspoon salt
½ to ¾ teaspoon curry powder

1 medium cucumber, peeled, seeded, halved lengthwise and cut into feed tube lengths

1 large celery stalk, peeled and cut into feed tube lengths
4 medium green onions, including green part, trimmed and cut into feed tube lengths

¾ pound cooked lamb, chopped
½ cup dried currants
Boston lettuce leaves

Bring 1 quart water to rapid boil over high heat. Add lentils. Reduce heat to medium-low, cover and simmer just until tender, about 20 minutes; do not overcook. Drain lentils and set aside.

Insert steel knife in processor. Mince parsley using on/off turns. Add apple and chop finely. Add oil, lemon juice, salt and curry. Blend until smooth, about 5 seconds. Do not empty work bowl.

Change to medium slicer blade. Slice cucumber, celery and green onion using light pressure.

Transfer mixture to large bowl. Add lentils, lamb and currants and toss to blend. Line salad bowl with lettuce leaves. Spoon lentil mixture into lettuce and serve immediately. *(Salad can be prepared up to 2 days ahead, covered and refrigerated. Transfer to lettuce-lined bowl just before serving.)*

❦ *Sandwiches*

Chicken-Apple Sandwiches

This is a perfect sandwich filling for pita bread halves.

Makes 6½ cups

4 chicken breast halves, skinned and boned
1 cup whipping cream

½ cup mayonnaise
½ cup sour cream
½ cup pecan halves

1 teaspoon dried tarragon, crumbled
½ teaspoon salt
Freshly ground pepper
3 pippin apples, cored and cut julienne

Preheat oven to 350°F. Arrange chicken in single layer in 9x5-inch loaf pan. Pour cream over. Bake until juices run clear when pierced with tip of sharp knife, about 30 minutes. Drain chicken; cool completely.

Combine mayonnaise, sour cream, pecans, tarragon, salt and pepper in large bowl. Shred chicken into 2-inch-long strips. Add chicken and apples to dressing and mix well. Cover and refrigerate overnight.

Bourbon Beef Sandwiches

3 to 4 servings

1 cup catsup
5 tablespoons Worcestershire sauce
6 tablespoons steak sauce
¾ cup chutney
¾ cup chili sauce
¼ teaspoon hot pepper sauce
½ cup bourbon

1 tablespoon butter
1 tablespoon vegetable oil
1 pound thinly sliced round steak
3 or 4 French bread rolls, halved

Combine first 7 ingredients in large bowl. Cover sauce and refrigerate overnight.

Pour sauce into saucepan. Cover and simmer 30 minutes.

Melt butter with oil in large skillet over high heat. Add meat in batches and brown well. Add meat to sauce and stir until heated through. Spoon onto rolls. Serve immediately. Pass remaining sauce separately.

Sausage and Bell Pepper Sandwich

6 servings

1½ pounds sweet Italian sausages, cut into ½-inch slices
½ cup water

2 large green bell peppers, seeded and cut into 1-inch pieces

2 medium onions, cut into 1-inch pieces
2 teaspoons dried oregano, crumbled
6 crusty French bread rolls, halved

Cook sausage in large skillet over medium heat until browned, about 10 minutes. Reduce heat to low, add water, cover and simmer 10 minutes.

Add bell peppers, onions and oregano to skillet and sauté until tender, about 10 minutes. Pour off liquid. Spoon sausage mixture into rolls and serve.

Open-face Quesadillas

A spicy, south-of-the-border open-face sandwich.

4 servings

3 egg whites
1 tablespoon red wine vinegar
12 ounces Monterey Jack cheese, cut into 1½-inch cubes
6 large green onions, including tops, cut into 1-inch pieces
1 serrano or jalapeño chili, halved and seeded
¼ to ½ teaspoon salt (depending on saltiness of cheese)
Freshly ground pepper

4 flour tortillas
1 small green bell pepper, cored, seeded and cut into thin rings
½ head romaine lettuce, shredded
1 medium avocado, peeled, pitted and sliced
½ cup Salsa Picante*
¼ cup sour cream

Place egg whites in processor work bowl and turn machine on. After 8 seconds, pour in vinegar and process until whites are whipped and hold their shape, about 45 seconds. Using rubber spatula, gently transfer whites to 1-quart mixing bowl; do not wash work bowl. Combine cheese, onions, serrano chili, salt and ground pepper in work bowl and blend 10 seconds, stopping once to scrape down sides of work bowl. Add ¼ of whites and mix using 2 on/off turns. Run spatula around inside of work bowl to loosen mixture. Spoon remaining whites onto cheese mixture and mix using 3 on/off turns. Run spatula around inside of work bowl. Mix using 1 more on/off turn just until combined; do not overprocess.

Position rack 6 inches from heat source and preheat broiler. Arrange tortillas on baking sheet. Divide green pepper rings among tortillas. Cover each with 6 tablespoons cheese mixture, spreading to edges. Broil until puffed and lightly browned, about 3 to 5 minutes. Top each quesadilla with shredded lettuce, then with avocado. Spoon on 2 tablespoons salsa and 1 tablespoon sour cream and serve.

*Salsa Picante

Makes about 2½ cups

½ cup cilantro leaves	3 tablespoons tomato paste
1 large garlic clove	1 teaspoon red wine vinegar
2 medium tomatoes, quartered	½ teaspoon salt
1 medium onion, quartered	¼ teaspoon sugar
1 to 2 serrano chilies, halved and seeded	

Place cilantro in processor work bowl. With machine running, drop garlic through feed tube and mince finely. Add tomatoes, onion and chilies and chop coarsely using 5 to 6 on/off turns. Add tomato paste, vinegar, salt and sugar and blend using 2 on/off turns. Transfer salsa to small bowl. Cover and refrigerate. Bring to room temperature before using.

Soft Tacos Grandes

Makes 8 tacos

6 ounces Monterey Jack or longhorn Colby cheese (well chilled), cut to fit feed tube	1 tablespoon red wine vinegar
½ head romaine lettuce, shredded	1 medium dried red chili (1 teaspoon flakes)
1 6¼-ounce can pitted colossal black olives, drained and sliced	¼ teaspoon cumin
	⅛ teaspoon oregano
	8 corn tortillas
1 15-ounce can pinto beans, drained and rinsed	1 cup Salsa Picante (see above)
	½ cup sour cream

Insert shredder blade in processor. Shred cheese using light pressure. Transfer to serving bowl. Place lettuce and olives in 2 other bowls.

Change to steel knife. Combine beans, vinegar, chili, cumin and oregano in work bowl and blend 15 seconds, stopping once to scrape down sides of bowl. Transfer mixture to small saucepan and warm through over low heat. To warm tortillas, set one at a time directly on electric burner or in preheated heavy skillet over low heat. Warm each tortilla about 1 minute, turning with tongs every 15 seconds; tortillas should be heated through but still pliable.

To serve, spread surface of tortilla with about 2 tablespoons hot bean mixture, adding cheese, lettuce and olives to taste. Top each with about 2 tablespoons Salsa Picante and 1 tablespoon sour cream. Carefully fold tortillas in half.

Rio Grande Fajitas

A quick and easy rendition of the popular southwestern soft rolled taco, accented with the flavorful salsa, Pico de Gallo.

6 servings

1 tablespoon freshly ground pepper
1 tablespoon garlic salt
½ teaspoon onion powder
½ teaspoon cayenne pepper
2 pounds tenderized beef skirt steaks, trimmed

12 8-inch flour tortillas, warmed
Pico de Gallo*
Guacamole

Combine first 4 ingredients and rub over meat. Cover and refrigerate meat overnight.

Prepare barbecue. Grill steaks to desired degree of doneness, turning frequently, about 5 minutes per side for well done. Slice across grain into thin strips. Divide among tortillas, placing strips in center of each. Top with Pico de Gallo and guacamole. Roll up. Serve hot.

Pico de Gallo

Makes 3½ cups

4 medium tomatoes, peeled
2 jalapeño chilies, roasted and peeled
½ onion, quartered

¼ cup fresh cilantro leaves
1 garlic clove, minced
¼ teaspoon salt

Combine all ingredients in processor and chop finely. Cover and refrigerate overnight.

2 🍃 Pasta, Vegetables, Eggs and Cheese

This chapter is full of great-tasting dishes that fit into a very contemporary way of dining—we might have once considered them only as first courses or as accompaniments to meats. But with today's focus on complex carbohydrates, vegetarian entrées and alternative sources of protein, more people are turning to pasta, vegetables, eggs or cheese as centerpiece dishes for lunches or suppers, dinner parties, brunches or buffets. And as you will see, these entrées can be anything from light to hearty.

Pasta, an all-time favorite, takes center stage with such recipes as Fusilli with Zucchini, Plum Tomatoes, Basil and Parsley (page 21), a colorful medley of pasta and fresh vegetables and herbs. For a truly elegant main course, Pasta with Scallops and Lemon Mustard Butter Sauce (page 22) and Florentine Lasagne Rolls with Shrimp Sauce (page 24) offer the added appeal of seafood and rich, flavorful sauces.

You don't need to be a vegetarian to enjoy the meatless dishes here. From wholesome Vegetarian Chili (page 25) and creamy Cheesy Zucchini Casserole (page 26) to an elegant Leek Tart with Cèpes (page 28) and exotic Tibetan Spicy Vegetable Cutlets (page 26), these imaginative main courses are both satisfying and delicious.

Eggs and cheese usually mean breakfast or brunch. With our interesting and wholesome variations, you'll be tempted to make them for lunch, as a good quick supper or for a special buffet. Try simple Spinach Baked Eggs (page 29) or Creamy Scrambled Eggs with Asparagus, Goat Cheese and Prosciutto (page 32). For a terrific party dish, make the Mexican-style Frittata (page 34) or Puffed Crab Omelet (page 34). For cheese lovers, there are rich, savory Chèvre and Roquefort cheesecakes (pages 37 and 38) or a Chicken Liver, Bacon and Cheese Quiche (page 36). Three-Cheese Pizza with Escarole and Garlic (page 39), made in a jelly roll pan, is ideal for a crowd.

Pasta

Pasta with Walnut Sauce

To make preparation quick and easy, use your food processor for chopping and grating, and cook the sauce in the microwave.

4 servings

2 cups milk
6 tablespoons (¾ stick) butter
¼ cup grated Swiss cheese
¼ cup freshly grated Parmesan cheese
¼ cup all purpose flour
1 teaspoon salt
¼ teaspoon freshly ground white pepper

2 tablespoons coarsely chopped walnuts
Freshly grated nutmeg
1 pound freshly cooked fusilli pasta
Additional freshly grated Parmesan cheese

Heat milk in large ovenproof glass bowl on High 2 minutes. Stir in butter, cheeses, flour, salt and pepper. Cook on High, stirring frequently, until slightly thickened, 4 to 5 minutes. Add walnuts and nutmeg and mix well. Add sauce to pasta and toss. Serve immediately, passing Parmesan separately.

Spaghetti with Asparagus, Almonds and Mushrooms

6 to 8 servings

¼ cup (½ stick) unsalted butter
2 large garlic cloves, minced
1 cup olive oil
1½ pounds asparagus, cut into 1-inch pieces
1½ cups sliced mushrooms
½ cup slivered almonds
1 teaspoon chopped fresh basil or ½ teaspoon dried, crumbled
1 teaspoon chopped fresh oregano or ½ teaspoon dried, crumbled

1 teaspoon chopped fresh thyme or ½ teaspoon dried, crumbled
½ teaspoon chopped fresh rosemary or ¼ teaspoon dried, crumbled
2 large tomatoes, peeled, seeded and diced
Salt and freshly ground pepper
1 pound spaghetti, freshly cooked
¼ cup freshly grated Parmesan cheese
¼ cup freshly grated Romano cheese

Melt butter in heavy large skillet over medium-low heat. Add garlic and cook until translucent, about 5 minutes. Add oil, asparagus, mushrooms, almonds, basil, oregano, thyme and rosemary and cook until asparagus is crisp-tender, stirring frequently, about 5 minutes. Mix in tomatoes. Season with salt and pepper. Remove from heat. Place pasta in large bowl. Pour vegetable mixture over and toss thoroughly. Sprinkle with Parmesan and Romano cheeses.

Rainbow Pasta Primavera

4 servings

1 cup freshly cooked Jerusalem artichoke rigatoni*
1 cup freshly cooked whole wheat pasta shells*
2 cups freshly cooked tricolored fusilli
2 large carrots, cut julienne, steamed until crisp-tender

½ cup broccoli florets, steamed until crisp-tender
¼ cup pitted black olives, chopped

2 cups whipping cream
½ cup freshly grated Parmesan cheese
2 tablespoons poppy seeds
Salt and freshly ground pepper

Combine pastas with carrots, broccoli and olives in large heatproof bowl. Keep warm.

Combine remaining ingredients in small saucepan over medium-low heat. Stir until sauce is slightly thickened, about 10 minutes. Pour over pasta mixture and toss. Serve immediately.

*Available at natural and specialty foods stores.

Confetti Pasta

4 to 6 servings

1½ cups chopped asparagus spears
¾ cup chopped crookneck squash
¾ cup diced red bell peppers
1 pound taglierini pasta, freshly cooked
¼ cup (½ stick) butter, melted
¼ cup freshly grated Parmesan cheese

9 ounces prosciutto, cut into bite-size pieces
Freshly grated nutmeg
Freshly ground pepper
Additional freshly grated Parmesan cheese

Steam asparagus until crisp-tender, 3 to 4 minutes. Drain well. Steam squash until crisp-tender, 1 to 2 minutes. Drain well. Steam bell peppers until crisp-tender, about 1 minute. Drain well. Place pasta on large serving platter. Top with butter and ¼ cup Parmesan and toss thoroughly. Add vegetables and prosciutto and toss. Season with nutmeg and pepper. Pass additional Parmesan separately.

Fettuccine with Prosciutto, Rosemary and Peas

4 servings

2 tablespoons olive oil
½ cup chopped onions
3 rosemary sprigs
2 garlic cloves, crushed
2 cups whipping cream
½ pound thinly sliced prosciutto, cut julienne

5 ounces tiny frozen peas, thawed
¾ pound fettuccine, freshly cooked
¼ cup freshly grated Parmesan cheese
Additional freshly grated Parmesan cheese

Heat oil in heavy large skillet over medium-high heat. Add onions, rosemary and garlic and cook until onions are translucent and garlic is brown, about 2 minutes. Discard garlic. Stir in cream. Increase heat and bring to boil. Reduce heat and simmer until sauce thickens, 6 minutes. Discard rosemary. Add prosciutto and peas to sauce and cook until heated through, about 1 minute. Place pasta in large bowl. Pour sauce over.

Fusilli with Zucchini, Plum Tomatoes, Basil and Parsley

6 servings

3 tablespoons olive oil
4 tablespoons freshly grated Parmesan cheese
½ pound small zucchini, trimmed and cut into ¼-inch-thick slices
½ pound ripe plum tomatoes, seeded and diced or 1¼ cups drained diced canned tomatoes
⅓ cup coarsely chopped fresh Italian parsley
¼ cup coarsely chopped fresh basil or 2 teaspoons dried, crumbled

2 medium shallots, minced
2 medium garlic cloves, minced
½ teaspoon dried marjoram, crumbled
½ teaspoon salt
½ teaspoon freshly ground pepper

½ pound fusilli or other short pasta
¼ cup chicken broth
1 tablespoon fresh lemon juice

Fresh basil leaves

Place 2 tablespoons oil on one small plate and 3 tablespoons Parmesan on another. Dip one side of each zucchini slice in oil, then in Parmesan. Arrange cheese side up on broiler pan. Combine tomatoes, parsley, chopped basil, shallots, garlic, marjoram, salt, pepper and remaining tablespoon oil in bowl.

Preheat broiler. Add fusilli to large pot of boiling salted water, stirring to prevent sticking. Cook until just tender but still firm to bite. Drain. Rinse with cold water; drain thoroughly. Add to tomato mixture. Mix in broth and lemon juice.

Broil zucchini 5 inches from heat source until bubbly and golden brown, about 3 minutes. Add to pasta and toss. Garnish with basil leaves. Sprinkle with remaining 1 tablespoon cheese. Serve at room temperature.

Pasta with Scallops and Lemon Mustard Butter Sauce

2 servings; can be doubled or tripled

1 cup dry white wine
½ teaspoon grated lemon peel
½ pound bay scallops
2 teaspoons Dijon mustard
¼ cup (½ stick) well-chilled butter, cut into 4 pieces
Salt and freshly ground pepper

5 ounces dried capellini or angel hair pasta
1 tablespoon butter
1 tablespoon snipped fresh chives

Bring wine and lemon peel to simmer in heavy medium skillet. Add scallops and cook until almost opaque, about 1 minute. Transfer scallops to bowl using slotted spoon. Increase heat and boil until wine is reduced to ¼ cup, about 6 minutes. Reduce heat to low. Whisk in mustard, then ¼ cup butter 1 piece at a time. Add scallops and any juices and heat through. Season with salt and freshly ground pepper.

Meanwhile, cook pasta in large pot of rapidly boiling salted water until just tender but still firm to bite. Drain well. Toss with 1 tablespoon butter. Divide between plates. Spoon scallops over. Sprinkle with chives.

Capellini with Zesty Crab Sauce

2 servings

1 tablespoon butter
½ cup chopped green onions
1 garlic clove, minced
2 medium tomatoes, peeled, seeded and chopped
¼ cup chicken broth
½ pound cooked crabmeat, shredded

1 tablespoon lemon juice
½ teaspoon celery salt
Freshly ground pepper
¼ cup chopped fresh parsley
4 ounces capellini, freshly cooked
Parsley sprigs

Melt butter in large skillet over medium heat. Add green onions and garlic. Stir until onions are tender, about 3 minutes. Add tomatoes and broth. Increase heat and bring to boil, stirring constantly. Reduce heat and simmer 2 minutes. Stir in crab, lemon juice, celery salt and pepper. Cook until heated through, about 2 minutes. Stir in chopped parsley. Mound pasta on serving platter. Stir in crab mixture. Garnish with parsley sprigs.

Tortellini in Bleu Cheese Sauce

4 servings

6 large dried shiitake mushrooms

2 tablespoons (¼ stick) butter
3 tablespoons bleu cheese, crumbled
3 tablespoons all purpose flour
1 tablespoon red currant jelly

1½ cups beef broth
1 pound prepared tortellini with chicken and veal filling, freshly cooked
Freshly grated Parmesan cheese

Cover mushrooms with warm water and let stand until softened, about 30 minutes. Drain mushrooms, reserving liquid. Squeeze dry. Coarsely chop, discarding stems.

Melt butter in heavy large saucepan over medium heat. Add bleu cheese and stir, pressing with back of wooden spoon, until cheese is melted (mixture may separate). Add flour and stir until golden, about 3 minutes. Stir in jelly until melted. Remove from heat. Combine reserved mushroom liquid and beef broth and whisk into cheese mixture. Stir over medium heat until thickened, about 6 minutes. Add mushrooms. Pour sauce over tortellini in heated serving dish and toss. Sprinkle with Parmesan and serve immediately.

Mushroom-stuffed Lasagne Rolls with Tomato Sauce

6 servings

Sauce
4 teaspoons olive oil
2 medium onions, chopped
2 medium garlic cloves, minced
1 medium red bell pepper, chopped
1 medium carrot, minced
1 teaspoon dried basil, crumbled
½ teaspoon dried marjoram, crumbled
½ teaspoon freshly ground pepper
¼ teaspoon dried rosemary, crumbled
½ cup dry white wine
1 1-pound can tomatoes, undrained
2 tablespoons tomato paste

Filling
1 tablespoon olive oil
½ pound mushrooms, coarsely chopped

1 large leek, trimmed and coarsely chopped
1 medium shallot, minced
1 medium garlic clove, minced
¼ teaspoon dried marjoram, crumbled
¼ teaspoon grated lemon peel
⅛ teaspoon dried rosemary, crumbled
⅛ teaspoon ground mace
⅛ teaspoon freshly ground pepper
8 tablespoons freshly grated Parmesan cheese
¼ teaspoon salt

6 lasagne noodles (preferably with ruffled edges)

For sauce: Heat oil in heavy large skillet over medium-high heat. Add onions, garlic, bell pepper, carrot, basil, marjoram, pepper and rosemary. Cook until vegetables are tender, stirring frequently, about 5 minutes. Add wine and boil until almost all liquid evaporates, about 5 minutes. Add tomatoes; break up large pieces with spoon. Mix in tomato paste. Reduce heat to low, cover and cook 45 minutes, stirring occasionally. Uncover and simmer until sauce thickens slightly, stirring frequently, about 10 minutes. *(Can be prepared 1 day ahead and refrigerated.)*

For filling: Heat oil in heavy large skillet over medium heat. Add mushrooms, leek, shallot, garlic, marjoram, lemon peel, rosemary, mace and pepper and stir 2 minutes. Reduce heat to low, cover and cook 30 minutes, stirring occasionally. Uncover and simmer until reduced to thick paste, stirring frequently, about 10 minutes. Mix in 5 tablespoons Parmesan and salt. Transfer to small bowl. Cover and refrigerate at least 20 minutes. *(Filling can be prepared 1 day ahead.)*

Preheat oven to 375°F. Cook noodles in boiling salted water until just tender but still firm to bite. Drain. Submerge in cold water. Spread half of tomato sauce over bottom of 9-inch square baking pan. Drain 1 noodle and pat dry. Place on work surface. Spread 3 tablespoons filling on noodle, leaving 1½-inch border at each end. Roll up jelly roll fashion. Arrange seam side down over sauce. Repeat with remaining noodles and filling, arranging noodles in pan so they just touch. Cover with foil and bake 25 minutes. Spoon remaining sauce decoratively over rolls. Cover and bake 20 minutes. Sprinkle with remaining 3 tablespoons Parmesan. Bake uncovered until cheese melts, about 5 minutes.

Florentine Lasagne Rolls with Shrimp Sauce

4 servings

Olive oil
2 10-ounce packages frozen chopped spinach, cooked and cooled
2 eggs
½ cup freshly grated Parmesan cheese
1 garlic clove, minced
½ teaspoon freshly grated nutmeg
½ teaspoon salt
¼ teaspoon freshly ground pepper

1 cup ricotta cheese
8 lasagne noodles, cooked
1½ tablespoons olive oil
9 ounces cooked bay shrimp
Leaf lettuce
4 large cooked shrimp, halved
2 cups Shrimp Sauce*
Freshly grated Parmesan cheese

Preheat oven to 350°F. Lightly coat 9x13-inch baking dish with olive oil. Combine spinach, 1 egg, ½ cup Parmesan, garlic, nutmeg, salt and pepper in large bowl. Mix ricotta with remaining egg in medium bowl. Pat 1 lasagne noodle dry with paper towel. Set on waxed paper. Brush with about ½ teaspoon olive oil. Spread about 3 tablespoons spinach mixture over noodle. Spread 2 tablespoons ricotta mixture over spinach. Pat about 12 bay shrimp onto ricotta. Carefully roll up noodle, starting at 1 short end, to enclose filling. Secure with toothpick. Transfer to prepared baking dish. Repeat with remaining noodles. *(Can be prepared 1 day ahead, covered tightly and refrigerated. Bring to room temperature before continuing.)* Bake 35 minutes. Garnish with lettuce and shrimp halves. Serve hot. Pass sauce and Parmesan separately.

*Shrimp Sauce

Makes about 2 cups

2 tablespoons (¼ stick) butter
1 teaspoon minced shallot
½ cup half and half
1 10¾-ounce can cream of shrimp soup

½ cup sour cream
3 ounces cooked bay shrimp
3 tablespoons Cream Sherry

Melt butter over medium heat in medium saucepan. Add shallot and sauté until limp. Pour in half and half and stir until bubbling. Add remaining ingredients to saucepan. Stir sauce until hot; do not boil.

 *Vegetables*

Garlic-scented Mixed Vegetable Sauté with Pecans

4 to 6 servings

2 medium leeks, white and light green parts only, halved lengthwise
2 medium celery stalks, peeled
1 medium red bell pepper
2 small zucchini
1 medium eggplant, trimmed

2 teaspoons vegetable oil
½ cup coarsely chopped pecans

Salt

9 tablespoons olive oil

Freshly ground pepper

5 garlic cloves, minced
7 teaspoons minced fresh oregano or 2 teaspoons dried, crumbled
2 tablespoons minced fresh parsley

Cut leeks into 2x¼-inch strips. Cut celery, pepper and zucchini into 2x¼-inch strips. Peel eggplant and cut into 2x½x¼-inch strips.

Heat vegetable oil in heavy small skillet over medium-low heat. Add pecans and pinch of salt. Stir until lightly browned, about 3 minutes. Set aside.

Heat 3 tablespoons olive oil in heavy large skillet over medium heat. Add eggplant and sprinkle with salt. Cook until just tender, tossing constantly, about 7 minutes. Transfer to bowl.

Heat 4 tablespoons olive oil in clean heavy large skillet over medium-low heat. Add leeks and celery and cook 5 minutes, stirring frequently. Add bell pepper, salt and freshly ground pepper. Cook until vegetables are almost tender, tossing frequently, about 5 minutes. Add zucchini and eggplant and toss until zucchini is crisp-tender, about 3 minutes. Transfer to platter.

Wipe skillet clean. Heat remaining 2 tablespoons olive oil over low heat. Add garlic and cook until just tender, about 30 seconds. Mix oregano and parsley into vegetables. Taste and adjust seasoning. Garnish with pecans and serve immediately.

Vegetarian Chili

6 servings

¼ cup vegetable oil
2 cups chopped onion
3¾ cups chopped tomatoes
3⅔ cups sliced mushrooms
2 cups broccoli florets
2 cups sliced zucchini
1 cup chopped green bell pepper
3 tablespoons chili powder
½ teaspoon garlic powder

⅛ teaspoon freshly ground pepper
¼ cup water
2 teaspoons all purpose flour
2 8¾-ounce cans red kidney beans, drained
3 cups freshly cooked rice
Sour cream
Chopped green onion
Shredded cheddar cheese

Heat oil in Dutch oven over medium-high heat. Add onion and sauté until translucent and slightly softened. Reduce heat to medium and add tomatoes, mushrooms, broccoli, zucchini, bell pepper, chili powder, garlic powder and pepper. Cover and simmer until vegetables are crisp-tender, about 10 minutes. Combine water and flour and stir into vegetable mixture. Add beans and cook until chili thickens, stirring frequently, about 5 minutes. Divide rice among bowls. Spoon chili over rice. Top with sour cream, green onion and cheese. Serve hot.

Spaghetti Squash with Olive, Anchovy and Caper Sauce

2 servings

1 small spaghetti squash (about 4x6 inches)

4 tablespoons (½ stick) butter
2 tablespoons olive oil
1 garlic clove, minced
1 6-ounce can pitted black olives, drained

½ cup fresh parsley
1 2-ounce can anchovies, rinsed and drained
1 teaspoon capers, drained
1 teaspoon fresh lemon juice

Salt and freshly ground pepper
Freshly grated Parmesan cheese

Place squash on rack in large saucepan. Add enough water to come just below squash. Bring to boil. Cover and steam until squash is slightly soft to touch, about 20 minutes. Cool; halve lengthwise. Scrape crosswise using large spoon to remove threads and seeds; discard. Scrape lengthwise to remove pastalike strands; set aside.

Melt 2 tablespoons butter with olive oil in heavy small skillet over low heat. Add garlic and stir 2 minutes. Mince olives, parsley, anchovies and capers with lemon juice in processor using on/off turns; do not process to paste. Add to skillet. Increase heat to medium and cook until heated through, stirring frequently, about 8 minutes.

Melt remaining butter in heavy medium skillet over medium-high heat. Add squash and toss until heated through. Season with salt and pepper. Transfer to plates. Spoon sauce over. Sprinkle with Parmesan and serve.

Spicy Vegetable Cutlets

Makes 10

1 cup cauliflower florets
1 cup diced peeled boiling potato
1 cup fresh green peas
1 cup sliced carrot
1 cup sliced green beans
2 teaspoons salt
½ teaspoon freshly ground pepper

4 eggs, beaten to blend
¼ cup all purpose flour
2 tablespoons minced fresh cilantro or parsley
1 cup toasted breadcrumbs
½ cup (or more) corn or peanut oil

Cook vegetables in boiling salted water until crisp-tender; do not overcook. Drain well. Puree vegetables in food processor with salt and pepper.

Line baking sheet with waxed paper. Shape about ½ cup vegetable mixture into ball. Flatten into egg-shaped cutlet about 1 inch thick. Set on prepared sheet. Repeat with remaining mixture. Refrigerate for 30 minutes.

Mix eggs, flour and cilantro in large bowl. Dip cutlets into batter, then coat evenly with breadcrumbs. Heat ½ cup oil in heavy large skillet over medium heat. Fry cutlets in batches until brown, about 2 minutes per side, adding more oil as necessary. Drain cutlets on paper towels and serve.

Cheesy Zucchini Casserole

6 servings

1½ cups freshly cooked rice
1 7-ounce can chopped mild green chilies, drained
6½ cups grated Monterey Jack cheese
3 medium zucchini, sliced and parboiled 6 minutes
1 large tomato, sliced

2 cups sour cream
2 tablespoons chopped green bell pepper
2 tablespoons chopped onion
1 tablespoon dried parsley, crumbled
1 teaspoon dried oregano, crumbled
1 teaspoon salt

Preheat oven to 350°F. Grease deep 2½-quart baking dish. Spread rice evenly in bottom of dish. Layer chilies, 5½ cups cheese, zucchini and tomato over rice. Combine sour cream, bell pepper, onion, parsley, oregano and salt. Spoon over zucchini mixture, lifting layers carefully to allow sour cream to mix in slightly. Sprinkle with remaining 1 cup grated Jack cheese. Bake 30 minutes. Serve casserole immediately.

Stuffed Eggplant with Almonds, Currants and Rice

This is a superb meatless main course, accented with an easy-to-make, curry-enhanced tomato sauce.

4 servings

Tomato Curry Sauce
- 2 tablespoons olive oil
- 2 garlic cloves, minced
- 1½ teaspoons curry powder
- 1½ pounds tomatoes, peeled, seeded and chopped
  Salt and freshly ground pepper
- 2 teaspoons tomato paste

Rice Pilaf
- 4 teaspoons vegetable oil
- ½ medium onion, minced
- ½ cup long-grain rice

- 1 cup hot water
- 3 tablespoons dried currants
  Salt and freshly ground pepper

- 2 medium eggplants (about 1 pound each), unpeeled, stems cut off, halved lengthwise
- 3 tablespoons olive oil

- 2 teaspoons vegetable oil
- ⅓ cup slivered almonds
- 1 tablespoon coarsely chopped fresh cilantro

For sauce: Heat oil in heavy large saucepan over low heat. Add garlic and cook, stirring occasionally, until soft, about 30 seconds. Add curry powder and stir 30 seconds. Mix in tomatoes, salt and pepper. Bring to boil, reduce heat to low and cook until tomatoes are very soft, stirring occasionally, about 30 minutes. Mix in tomato paste. Puree in processor until smooth. Adjust seasoning. *(Can be prepared 1 day ahead. Cover and refrigerate.)*

For pilaf: Heat 4 teaspoons vegetable oil in medium skillet over low heat. Add onion and cook until soft, stirring frequently, about 10 minutes. Add rice and stir until milky white, about 2 minutes. Add water, currants, salt and pepper. Bring to boil, stir once and cover. Reduce heat to low and cook until tender, about 18 minutes. Remove mixture from heat and let stand covered for 10 minutes.

Preheat oven to 450°F. Lightly grease shallow baking dish. Make ⅛-inch-deep cut around edge of each eggplant half. Score 3 times down center. Arrange eggplants cut side up in prepared dish. Sprinkle surface with salt and 2 tablespoons olive oil. Bake until eggplant is tender when pierced with knife, about 25 minutes. Cool slightly.

Remove eggplant pulp from skins using spoon; do not pierce skin. Pat skins dry. Coarsely chop pulp and add to pilaf. Taste and adjust seasoning. *(Can be prepared 1 day ahead and refrigerated. Bring to room temperature before continuing.)*

Heat 2 teaspoons vegetable oil in heavy small skillet over medium-low heat. Add almonds and pinch of salt. Stir until light brown, about 2 minutes. Stir almonds into rice pilaf with cilantro.

Preheat oven to 350°F. Oil individual baking dishes or 1 large baking dish. Place eggplants cut side up in dishes. Spoon pilaf into eggplant shells. Sprinkle with remaining 1 tablespoon olive oil. Bake until pilaf is hot, about 15 minutes. Reheat sauce in heavy medium saucepan, stirring frequently. Spoon sauce around eggplant or divide sauce among plates and top with eggplant. Serve immediately.

Leek Tart with Cèpes

The delicately balanced flavors make this a very special tart.

4 servings

Yeast Dough
  1 **envelope dry yeast**
  ¼ **cup warm water (105°F to 115°F)**
  1¾ **cups (about) unbleached all purpose flour**
  2 **eggs, room temperature**
  ¾ **teaspoon salt**
  ¼ **cup (½ stick) unsalted butter, cut into 8 pieces, room temperature**

Leek Filling
  1 **ounce dried cèpes**
  2 **pounds leeks (white and light green parts only), halved lengthwise**

  3 **tablespoons unsalted butter**
    Salt and freshly ground pepper

  ¾ **cup plus 2 tablespoons whipping cream**
  2 **eggs**
  1 **egg yolk**
    Freshly grated nutmeg

  ¼ **cup grated Gruyère cheese**

For dough: Sprinkle yeast onto warm water in small bowl; stir to dissolve. Let stand 10 minutes. Sift 1½ cups flour into bowl of heavy-duty mixer fitted with dough hook. Add yeast mixture, eggs and salt. Mix at medium speed until blended and dough begins to cling to hook, stopping occasionally to scrape down sides of bowl, about 7 minutes. If dough is wet, beat in remaining flour 1 tablespoon at a time until soft dough forms. Continue mixing until dough is smooth, clings to hook and almost cleans sides of bowl, stopping once to scrape down sides of bowl, about 5 minutes. Mix in half of butter until blended, then repeat with remaining butter, mixing until soft and slightly sticky dough forms.

Lightly oil medium bowl. Add dough, turning to coat entire surface. Cover bowl with plastic wrap. Let dough rise in warm draft-free area until doubled in volume, about 1 hour.

For filling: Soak cèpes in hot water to cover until tender, about 20 minutes. Transfer to strainer; rinse and drain well. Cut cèpes into ¼-inch pieces, discarding hard core. Cut leeks crosswise into ¼-inch-thick slices.

Melt butter in heavy large skillet over low heat. Add leeks, salt and pepper. Cover and cook 15 minutes, stirring frequently. Add cèpes, cover and cook until leeks are very soft, stirring occasionally, about 5 minutes. Uncover and stir over medium-high heat until liquid evaporates. Let cool.

Whisk cream, eggs, yolk, salt, pepper and nutmeg in large bowl. Mix in leeks. Taste and adjust seasoning.

Position rack in center of oven and preheat to 425°F. Butter 9-inch round fluted tart pan with removable bottom. Lift dough and let fall into bowl 3 times to eliminate air pockets. Transfer dough to prepared pan. Oil knuckles and push dough outward from center to line pan. Push against rim of pan with oiled fingers to form ½-inch-thick edge. Set tart pan on baking sheet. Ladle leek mixture into tart. Gently push edge of dough up above pan rim. Sprinkle dough with cheese. Let stand in draft-free area about 10 minutes.

Bake tart 15 minutes. Reduce oven temperature to 350°F and continue baking until filling is light brown and just firm to touch, about 25 minutes. Cool on rack 15 minutes. Serve warm or at room temperature. *(Can be prepared up to 4 hours ahead.)*

Eggs

Poached Eggs with Tarragon Mushroom Sauce

6 servings

Butter
½ cup (1 stick) butter
1 pound mushrooms, sliced
1 garlic clove, minced
Salt and freshly ground pepper
1 tablespoon dry Sherry
¾ teaspoon dried tarragon, crumbled

¼ cup all purpose flour
2 cups milk

¾ cup grated Swiss cheese
12 poached eggs

Preheat broiler. Butter six 5- to 6-inch gratin dishes. Melt ¼ cup butter in heavy large skillet over medium heat. Add mushrooms and cook until most of juices have evaporated, about 10 minutes. Add garlic. Season with salt and pepper. Cook until garlic softens, about 5 minutes. Add Sherry and tarragon. Increase heat to high and cook until liquid evaporates, 2 to 3 minutes. Set mushroom mixture aside.

Melt remaining ¼ cup butter in heavy large saucepan over medium-low heat. Add flour and stir until mixture is smooth and bubbly. Remove from heat and stir in milk. Set pan over medium-high heat and boil 1 minute, stirring constantly. Reduce heat to medium and cook 10 minutes, stirring often. Season with salt and pepper.

Preheat broiler. Stir mushroom mixture into sauce. Add ½ cup cheese and stir over low heat until melted. Divide eggs among prepared dishes. Spoon some of sauce into each dish. Top each with some of remaining cheese. Broil until cheese is melted and bubbly. Serve immediately.

Spinach Baked Eggs

2 to 4 servings

3 pounds fresh spinach,* stemmed

3 tablespoons butter
Freshly grated nutmeg
¾ cup whipping cream
Salt and freshly ground pepper

4 eggs
¼ cup shredded Gruyère cheese

Cook spinach in large saucepan of boiling salted water until just tender, about 2 minutes. Rinse and drain well. Gently squeeze dry. Chop coarsely.

Melt butter in heavy large skillet over low heat. Add spinach and nutmeg and stir until butter is absorbed, about 2 minutes. Add ½ cup cream and simmer until absorbed, about 3 minutes. Season with salt and pepper. *(Can be prepared 1 day ahead and refrigerated.)*

Position rack in center of oven and preheat to 400°F. Butter four 6-inch shallow baking dishes or two 8x1-inch round dishes. Heat in oven until hot, 2 minutes.

Meanwhile, reheat spinach mixture over medium-low heat until very hot, stirring constantly. Divide among hot dishes. Make well in center of each small dish, using small spoon, or make 2 wells in each large dish. Break 1 egg into small bowl and then slide into well, being careful not to break yolk; repeat, adding 1 egg to each well. Spoon 1 tablespoon cream over each egg. Sprinkle with cheese. For very soft eggs, bake 5 minutes for small dishes or 6 minutes for large. Check and continue cooking until eggs are set as desired. Serve immediately.

*Two 10-ounce packages frozen leaf spinach can be substituted. Thaw, squeeze dry and chop coarsely. Do not precook.

Baked Eggs with Chicken in Tarragon Cream Sauce

4 servings

2 cups rich chicken stock, preferably homemade
½ pound boned chicken breasts, skinned and cut into thin strips
6 ounces mushrooms, halved and thinly sliced
Salt and freshly ground white pepper

1 cup whipping cream
1 tablespoon minced fresh tarragon or 1 teaspoon dried, crumbled

4 eggs
2 teaspoons minced fresh tarragon or parsley

Preheat oven to 400°F. Heat stock to simmer in large saucepan. Stir in chicken, mushrooms, salt and pepper. Cover, reduce heat to low and cook until chicken is just tender, about 3 minutes. Transfer chicken and mushrooms to bowl using slotted spoon. Boil stock until reduced to ⅓ cup, stirring occasionally, about 15 minutes. Add cream and boil until thickened, stirring frequently, about 4 minutes. Return chicken and mushrooms to sauce using slotted spoon; discard any liquid in bowl. Stir in 1 tablespoon tarragon. Taste and adjust seasoning.

Meanwhile, arrange four 1-cup ramekins in roasting pan or large shallow baking dish. Pour boiling water into roasting pan to come halfway up sides of ramekins. Heat in oven until ramekins are hot, about 2 minutes.

Divide hot chicken and mushrooms equally among ramekins using slotted spoon. Add 1 tablespoon sauce to each ramekin. Make well in center of each with small spoon. Break 1 egg into small bowl and then slide into well, being careful not to break yolk; repeat, adding 1 egg to each well. Spoon 2 tablespoons sauce over each egg. Bake in water bath 9 minutes for very soft eggs. Check and continue cooking until eggs are set as desired. Carefully dry ramekins and set on plates. Sprinkle with tarragon. Serve immediately.

Baked Eggs with Tomatoes and Kashkavàl Cheese

2 to 4 servings

1 tablespoon butter
1 garlic clove, minced
2½ pounds tomatoes, peeled, seeded and chopped
1 bay leaf
¼ teaspoon dried thyme, crumbled
Salt and freshly ground pepper

4 eggs
4 tablespoons (½ stick) butter, melted
6 tablespoons grated kashkavàl or Parmesan cheese

Melt 1 tablespoon butter in heavy large skillet over low heat. Add garlic and stir 30 seconds. Add tomatoes, bay leaf, thyme, salt and pepper and bring to boil. Reduce heat to medium and cook until tomatoes are soft and mixture is thick, stirring frequently, about 20 minutes. Discard bay leaf. Taste and adjust seasoning. *(Can be prepared 2 days ahead. Cover and refrigerate.)*

Position rack in center of oven and preheat to 425°F. Butter four 6-inch shallow baking dishes or one 8x1-inch round dish. Heat in oven until hot, 2 minutes.

Meanwhile, reheat tomato mixture over medium-low heat until very hot, stirring frequently. Divide among small dishes or spread in bottom of large dish. Make well in center of each dish using small spoon, or make 4 wells in large dish. Break 1 egg into small bowl and then slide into well, being careful not to break yolk; repeat, adding 1 egg to each well. Spoon 1 tablespoon melted butter over each egg and sprinkle whites with cheese. For very soft eggs, bake 5 minutes for small dishes or 6 minutes for large dish. Check and continue cooking until eggs are set as desired. Set dishes on plates and serve eggs immediately.

Steelers' Brunch

8 to 10 servings

¼ cup (½ stick) butter
18 eggs
1 cup sour cream
1 cup milk
¼ cup chopped onion
Salt

2 tablespoons (¼ stick) butter
½ pound mushrooms
2 tablespoons dry white wine
2 teaspoons fresh lemon juice
Salt and freshly ground pepper

Preheat oven to 325°F. Melt ¼ cup butter in 9x13-inch baking dish. Combine eggs, sour cream, milk, onion and salt in large bowl and beat until light and foamy. Pour into dish. Bake until tester inserted in center comes out clean, about 35 minutes.

Meanwhile, melt remaining butter in medium skillet over medium-high heat. Add mushrooms and sauté until liquid is evaporated, about 5 minutes. Add remaining ingredients and continue to cook, stirring constantly, until liquid is reduced by half. Arrange mushrooms over eggs. Cut into squares and serve.

Eggs Mexicanos

4 servings

1 tablespoon vegetable oil
3 corn tortillas, cut into wedges
¼ cup chopped onion
4 eggs, beaten to blend

¼ teaspoon salt
½ cup shredded Monterey Jack cheese
Salsa

Heat oil in large skillet over high heat. Add tortilla wedges and fry until crisp, about 2 minutes. Add onion and stir 1 minute. Reduce heat to medium. Add eggs and salt and stir until eggs begin to set. Add cheese. Continue stirring until cheese melts and eggs are set. Serve hot, passing salsa separately.

Creamy Scrambled Eggs with Asparagus, Goat Cheese and Prosciutto

4 servings

12 medium asparagus spears, peeled and cut into ½-inch pieces

10 eggs

¼ cup whipping cream
Salt and freshly ground white pepper

2 tablespoons (¼ stick) unsalted butter

½ cup diced goat cheese (preferably Montrachet)

1 tablespoon minced fresh chives

2 tablespoons (¼ stick) unsalted butter

2 thin slices prosciutto, cut into 2½x1½-inch strips

Boil asparagus in enough salted water to cover until just tender when pierced with sharp knife, about 2 minutes. Drain. Rinse asparagus thoroughly under cold water; drain again and set aside.

Whisk eggs with cream, salt and pepper in large bowl until blended. Melt 2 tablespoons butter in heavy 3-quart saucepan over low heat. Add eggs and cook, stirring constantly with wooden spoon or whisk and scraping eggs from bottom and sides of pan, until eggs begin to thicken and tiny curds form, 20 to 25 minutes. Eggs should be soft and creamy, slightly thicker than a sauce and slightly firmer than creamed cottage cheese; do not overcook. If firmer consistency is desired, continue stirring until cooked to desired doneness.

Remove from heat and mix in goat cheese and chives. Spoon eggs into shallow bowl. Set bowl in warm water bath to keep eggs hot.

Melt butter in medium skillet over medium heat. Add asparagus and sauté 1 minute. Remove 8 asparagus tips and reserve for garnish. Add prosciutto to asparagus in skillet and stir until heated through, about 15 seconds. Gently stir asparagus mixture into eggs. Garnish with reserved asparagus tips. Serve immediately.

Creamy Scrambled Eggs with Smoked Turkey, Dill Butter and Peas

4 servings

¼ cup (½ stick) unsalted butter, room temperature

1 tablespoon snipped fresh dill
Freshly ground pepper

10 eggs

¼ cup whipping cream
Salt and freshly ground white pepper

2 tablespoons (¼ stick) unsalted butter

⅔ cup cooked peas

2 ounces thinly sliced smoked turkey, cut into 1¾x½-inch strips

Cream butter until smooth. Add dill and pepper and beat until well blended. Cover and refrigerate at least 30 minutes to blend flavors. *(Can be prepared 2 days ahead and chilled. Bring to room temperature before using.)*

Whisk eggs with cream, salt and pepper in large bowl until blended. Melt 2 tablespoons butter in heavy 3-quart saucepan over low heat. Add eggs and cook, stirring constantly with wooden spoon or whisk and scraping eggs from bottom and sides of pan, until eggs begin to thicken and tiny curds form, 20 to 25 minutes. Eggs should be soft and creamy, slightly thicker than a sauce and slightly firmer than creamed cottage cheese; do not overcook. If firmer consistency is desired, continue stirring until cooked to desired doneness.

Remove from heat and stir in 2 tablespoons dill butter. Spoon eggs into shallow bowl. Set bowl in warm water bath to keep eggs hot.

Melt remaining dill butter in heavy medium skillet over low heat. Add peas and stir until heated through, about 2 minutes. Add turkey and stir until heated through, about 30 seconds. Gently blend pea mixture into eggs. Adjust seasoning and serve.

Southwestern-style Scrambled Eggs with Shrimp and Corn

4 servings

10 eggs
¼ cup whipping cream
   Salt and freshly ground white pepper
2 tablespoons (¼ stick) unsalted butter

6 ounces small uncooked shrimp, shelled and deveined

2 tablespoons (¼ stick) unsalted butter
1 small garlic clove, minced
½ jalapeño chili, seeded and minced
   Salt
½ cup cooked corn
½ cup grated Monterey Jack cheese
1 tablespoon chopped cilantro

Whisk eggs with cream, salt and pepper in large bowl until blended. Melt 2 tablespoons butter in heavy 3-quart saucepan over low heat. Add eggs and cook, stirring constantly with wooden spoon or whisk and scraping eggs from bottom and sides of pan, until eggs begin to thicken and tiny curds form, 20 to 25 minutes. Eggs should be soft and creamy, slightly thicker than a sauce and slightly firmer than creamed cottage cheese; do not overcook. If firmer consistency is desired, continue stirring until cooked to desired doneness.

Remove from heat and spoon eggs into shallow bowl. Set in warm water bath to keep eggs hot.

Set aside 8 shrimp for garnish. Chop remaining shrimp. Melt butter in heavy medium skillet over medium heat. Add whole and chopped shrimp, garlic, jalapeño and salt and sauté until shrimp are opaque, about 1½ minutes. Remove whole shrimp; set aside. Add corn to skillet and stir until heated through. Blend cheese into eggs. Gently stir shrimp mixture and cilantro into eggs. Adjust seasoning. Garnish with reserved shrimp.

Bacon-Cheese Oven Omelet

6 servings

4 ounces Swiss cheese, thinly sliced
7 bacon slices
8 eggs, beaten to blend

1 cup milk
   Salt and freshly ground pepper
   Italian parsley

Preheat oven to 350°F. Lightly butter 9-inch round baking dish. Arrange cheese slices in bottom. Cook bacon in large skillet over low heat until done but still flexible. Drain well on paper towels. Chop 4 slices; halve remaining 3 slices crosswise and curl each into spiral. Whisk eggs and milk. Season with salt and pepper. Stir in chopped bacon. Pour over cheese. Bake 25 minutes. Place parsley in center of omelet. Arrange bacon curls around edge. Bake 5 more minutes. Cool 5 minutes. Serve hot.

Mexican-style Frittata

2 servings

1 tablespoon butter
½ cup minced onions
2 to 3 jalapeño chilies, seeded and finely chopped
2 large tomatoes, diced

5 eggs, beaten to blend
6 ounces cheddar cheese, grated

¼ cup chopped fresh cilantro
Salt and freshly ground pepper
2 tablespoons (¼ stick) butter

Fresh cilantro sprigs

Melt 1 tablespoon butter in heavy small skillet over medium-low heat. Add onions and chilies and cook until tender, stirring occasionally, about 5 minutes. Stir in tomatoes and cook until softened, stirring occasionally, 3 minutes. Cool slightly.

Transfer tomato mixture to medium bowl. Add eggs, cheese, ¼ cup cilantro and salt and pepper. Melt 2 tablespoons butter in heavy 9-inch ovenproof skillet over medium heat. Add egg mixture. Pierce holes in egg mixture and lift edges with spatula, tipping pan to allow uncooked egg to flow under, until edge forms, about 1 minute; do not stir. Reduce heat to low. Cover skillet and continue cooking until eggs are almost set, about 5 minutes.

Meanwhile, preheat broiler. Uncover skillet and broil frittata until eggs are set and top is golden brown, watching carefully. Garnish with cilantro sprigs.

Puffed Crab Omelet

This is delicious served hot or at room temperature. If reheated as directed, it will puff a second time.

6 to 8 servings

Omelet
Butter
All purpose flour
1 cup (2 sticks) unsalted butter
1 cup all purpose flour
2 cups milk
8 eggs, beaten to blend
½ teaspoon salt
¼ teaspoon freshly grated nutmeg

Filling
¾ pound cooked crabmeat
1⅓ cups (about) whipping cream

2 tablespoons (¼ stick) unsalted butter
2 tablespoons all purpose flour
2 tablespoons dry Sherry
Salt
Cayenne pepper

Lemon slices
Fresh dill

For omelet: Preheat oven to 400°F. Butter jelly roll pan; line with waxed paper. Butter and flour paper. Melt 1 cup butter in heavy medium saucepan over medium-low heat. Whisk in flour and cook 3 minutes. Increase heat, whisk in milk and cook until thick and smooth, about 2 minutes. Remove from heat. Beat in eggs, salt and nutmeg. Pour batter into prepared pan. Bake until omelet is puffed and golden, 20 to 30 minutes.

Meanwhile, prepare filling: Drain any crab liquid into measuring cup. Add enough cream to equal 1⅓ cups. Melt butter in heavy medium saucepan over medium-low heat. Whisk in flour and cook 3 minutes. Whisk in cream mixture and boil until thick and smooth, about 2 minutes. Add Sherry and boil 1 minute. Add crab and heat through. Season with salt and cayenne.

Line work surface with waxed paper. Invert omelet onto paper. Remove paper from bottom of omelet. Spread omelet with ¾ of filling. Starting at short end and using paper as aid, roll omelet up as for jelly roll. Transfer to platter. Garnish with lemon and dill. *(Can be prepared 1 hour ahead. Reheat in 400° F oven for 5 to 8 minutes.)*

Hash Frittata

4 servings

2 tablespoons vegetable oil
1 medium potato, peeled and cut julienne
1 medium onion, thinly sliced
¼ cup finely chopped green bell pepper

¾ cup chopped, cooked steak, roast beef, turkey or chicken
8 eggs, beaten to blend

Heat oil in large nonstick skillet over medium heat. Add potato, onion and bell pepper. Cover and cook until tender, stirring occasionally, about 10 minutes. Sprinkle meat evenly over vegetables. Pour eggs over. Cook until eggs are set on bottom and beginning to firm on top, 4 to 5 minutes. Place lightly greased rimless baking sheet over skillet. Holding firmly, quickly flip skillet to invert frittata onto sheet. Slide frittata back into skillet. Continue cooking until set on bottom, about 3 minutes.

 # *Cheese*

Sausage Cheese Casserole

4 to 6 servings

1 pound link sausages
1 29-ounce can whole tomatoes, drained (reserve liquid) and chopped
½ pound elbow macaroni
¼ cup (½ stick) butter or margarine

1 medium onion, chopped
½ cup water
2 teaspoons salt
1 teaspoon Worcestershire sauce
¼ teaspoon freshly ground pepper
2 cups shredded sharp cheddar cheese

Brown sausages well in heavy large skillet over medium-high heat. Drain excess fat. Chop sausages into ¾-inch pieces. Return to skillet. Add tomatoes and reserved liquid, macaroni, butter, onion, water, salt, Worcestershire sauce and pepper. Simmer, stirring frequently, until macaroni is tender, about 20 to 25 minutes. Stir in cheese. Continue simmering until cheese melts. Serve hot.

Jalapeño Cheese Pie

8 to 10 servings

¾ cup diced jalapeño chilies, seeded
¾ pound cheddar cheese, grated
¾ pound Monterey Jack cheese, grated
¼ teaspoon salt

Pinch of garlic powder
Dash of Worcestershire sauce
¼ cup diced onion
12 eggs, beaten to blend

Preheat oven to 300°F. Lightly butter 9x13-inch baking dish. Spread ½ cup chilies evenly over bottom of dish. Add cheeses and press firmly to form crust. Sprinkle with salt, garlic powder and Worcestershire sauce. Top with onion and remaining chilies. Spread eggs evenly over. Bake until partially set, about 25 to 30 minutes. Turn off oven, open door and let pie cool 10 minutes to set. Cut Jalapeño Cheese Pie evenly into squares and serve warm or chilled.

Green Chili Brunch Quiche

Use the microwave to prepare this quick and easy entrée.

6 servings

1½ cups shredded Monterey Jack cheese (about 4 ounces)
1 cup shredded cheddar cheese (about 3 ounces)
1 9-inch pie shell, baked (in glass or ceramic pie plate)

1 4-ounce can diced green chilies
1 cup half and half
¼ teaspoon salt
¼ teaspoon cumin powder
3 eggs, lightly beaten

Sprinkle Monterey Jack cheese and half of cheddar cheese evenly over pie shell. Reserve 2 tablespoons chilies for topping; sprinkle remaining chilies evenly over cheese. Combine half and half, salt and cumin in 1-quart microwave-safe bowl. Cook on High, stirring occasionally, until mixture thickens, about 2½ to 3 minutes; *do not boil.* Slowly whisk cream mixture into eggs, blending thoroughly. Pour into pie shell. Sprinkle with remaining cheddar cheese and chilies. Cook on Medium (50 percent power) until set, about 12 to 13 minutes, turning dish halfway through cooking time. Transfer quiche to broiler and cook briefly to brown top lightly. Let stand 2 to 3 minutes. Cut into wedges and serve.

Chicken Liver, Bacon and Cheese Quiche

6 to 8 servings

1 9-inch pie shell
2 tablespoons Dijon mustard

2 tablespoons (¼ stick) butter
6 large mushrooms, sliced
1 small onion, thinly sliced
⅓ pound chicken livers, sliced and patted dry
⅓ cup sour cream
2 tablespoons dry Sherry

Salt and freshly ground pepper
2 slices bacon, cooked and crumbled
½ cup grated cheddar cheese
3 tablespoons grated Romano cheese
3 eggs, room temperature
1½ cups whipping cream
⅛ teaspoon cayenne pepper
⅛ teaspoon sugar
⅛ teaspoon freshly ground pepper

Preheat oven to 425°F. Brush shell with mustard. Bake 5 minutes. Remove shell from oven; retain temperature.

Melt butter in heavy medium saucepan over medium-high heat. Add mushrooms and onion and sauté until just tender, about 1 minute. Add livers and sauté 1 minute. Reduce heat to low, cover and cook 15 minutes. Blend in sour cream and Sherry and stir until mixture is heated through. Season with salt and pepper. Spoon mixture into crust. Sprinkle with bacon and grated cheeses. Whip eggs lightly in blender. Add cream, cayenne, sugar and ⅛ teaspoon pepper and blend well. Pour over cheese. Bake 15 minutes. Reduce oven to 400°F and continue baking until tester inserted in center comes out clean, about 20 minutes. Let quiche cool 5 minutes before serving.

Potato Cheese Soufflé

4 servings

1 pound boiling potatoes, peeled
1 ounce Parmesan cheese, grated (¼ cup)
¼ cup whipping cream
1 tablespoon unsalted butter, melted
3 eggs, separated

¼ pound Gruyère cheese, grated (1 cup)
¾ teaspoon salt
⅛ teaspoon freshly grated nutmeg
Pinch of cayenne pepper

Cook potatoes in boiling salted water until very tender. Drain. Puree through food mill or sieve into bowl (about 1⅓ cups packed puree). *Do not use processor.*

Preheat oven to 400°F. Generously butter 4-cup soufflé dish. Sprinkle bottom and sides with 1 tablespoon Parmesan. Stir cream and butter into potato puree. Mix in yolks, Gruyère, salt, nutmeg and pepper. Beat whites with pinch of salt until stiff but not dry. Fold ¼ of whites into potato mixture to lighten. Fold in remaining whites. Spoon into prepared dish. Bake until puffed, set and golden, 25 to 30 minutes.

Gruyère Torte

8 to 12 servings

1½ tablespoons butter (for pan)
½ cup fine French breadcrumbs, lightly toasted
¼ cup finely grated Gruyère cheese

2 cups small curd cottage cheese
¼ cup all purpose flour

¾ teaspoon salt
⅛ teaspoon cayenne pepper
4 eggs
1 cup whipping cream
½ pound Gruyère cheese, grated
Freshly grated nutmeg

Preheat oven to 350°F. Butter bottom and ⅔ up sides of 9-inch springform pan. Mix breadcrumbs and ¼ cup Gruyère. Sprinkle mixture into prepared pan, turning to coat sides. Refrigerate.

Mix cottage cheese in blender or processor until smooth. Blend in flour, salt and cayenne pepper. With machine running, add eggs, then cream and cheese. Season with nutmeg. Pour into prepared pan. Set pan in roasting pan. Add enough hot water to come halfway up sides of springform. Bake 1 hour. Cool slightly. Serve warm.

Chèvre Cheesecake

12 servings

1½ tablespoons butter (for pan)
⅓ cup breadcrumbs, lightly toasted
¼ cup ground walnuts
¼ cup freshly grated Parmesan cheese

1½ pounds cream cheese, room temperature

½ pound chèvre (such as Bûcheron or Montrachet)
4 eggs
½ cup whipping cream
½ teaspoon salt

Preheat oven to 325°F. Butter 9-inch springform pan. Mix breadcrumbs, nuts and Parmesan. Sprinkle into pan, turning to coat. Refrigerate.

Mix cream cheese and chèvre in blender or processor. Add remaining ingredients and blend until smooth. Pour into prepared pan. Set pan in roasting pan. Add enough hot water to come halfway up sides of springform. Bake 1 hour and 20 minutes. Turn oven off and cool cheesecake about 1 hour with door ajar. Transfer to rack. Cool to room temperature before removing from pan and serving.

Roquefort Cheesecake

12 servings

1½ tablespoons butter (for pan)
½ cup breadcrumbs, lightly toasted
¼ cup freshly grated Parmesan cheese

½ pound sliced bacon
1 medium onion, minced

1¾ pounds cream cheese, room temperature

½ pound Roquefort cheese
4 eggs
⅓ cup whipping cream
½ teaspoon salt
2 or 3 drops hot pepper sauce

Preheat oven to 325°F. Butter 9-inch springform pan. Mix breadcrumbs and Parmesan. Sprinkle mixture in pan, turning to coat. Refrigerate.

Fry bacon in heavy medium skillet until crisp. Remove from pan using tongs and drain on paper towel. Pour off all but about 1 tablespoon bacon fat from skillet. Add onion. Cover and cook over low heat until translucent, stirring occasionally, about 10 minutes. Set aside.

Crumble bacon. Mix cream cheese and Roquefort in blender or processor until smooth. Add eggs, cream, salt and pepper sauce and process until smooth. Blend in bacon and onion; filling should retain some texture. Pour into prepared pan. Set pan in roasting pan. Add enough hot water to come halfway up sides of springform. Bake 1 hour and 20 minutes. Turn oven off and cool cheesecake about 1 hour with door ajar. Transfer to rack. Cool to room temperature before removing from pan and serving.

Smoked Salmon Cheesecake

12 servings

1½ tablespoons butter (for pan)
½ cup fine French breadcrumbs, lightly toasted
¼ cup finely grated Gruyère cheese
1 teaspoon minced fresh dill or ¼ to ½ teaspoon dried

3 tablespoons butter
1 medium onion, minced

1¾ pounds cream cheese, room temperature
4 eggs
½ cup grated Gruyère cheese
⅓ cup half and half
½ teaspoon salt
½ pound smoked salmon, coarsely chopped

Preheat oven to 325°F. Butter 9-inch springform pan. Mix breadcrumbs, ¼ cup Gruyère and dill. Sprinkle into pan, turning to coat. Refrigerate.

Melt butter in heavy medium skillet over low heat. Add onion, cover and cook until translucent, about 10 minutes, stirring occasionally. Mix cream cheese in blender or processor until smooth. Add eggs, remaining Gruyère, half and half and salt and mix until smooth. Blend in onion and salmon; filling should retain some texture.

Pour into prepared pan. Set pan in roasting pan. Add enough hot water to come halfway up sides of springform. Bake 1 hour and 20 minutes. Turn oven off and cool cheesecake about 1 hour with door ajar. Transfer to rack. Cool to room temperature before removing from pan and serving.

Three-Cheese Pizza with Escarole and Garlic

6 servings

Cornmeal

8 quarts water
Salt
2 pounds escarole, thick center ribs removed

4 large garlic cloves
5 tablespoons olive oil (preferably extra-virgin)

¾ teaspoon salt
Freshly ground pepper

5 ounces mozzarella cheese, cut into 1-inch pieces
5 ounces Asiago cheese, cut into 1-inch pieces

1½ pounds Whole Wheat Pizza Dough*

½ cup ricotta cheese, well drained

Position rack in center of oven. Set baking stone or baking tiles on rack if available. Preheat oven to 475°F. Oil bottom and sides of 11½x17½-inch jelly roll pan (preferably black steel). Sprinkle pan with cornmeal.

Bring 8 quarts salted water to boil in large pot. Add escarole and cook 3 minutes. Drain; rinse under cold water. Drain well. Wrap escarole in towel and squeeze to remove excess moisture. Set aside.

Insert steel knife in processor. With machine running, drop garlic through feed tube and mince. Heat 4 tablespoons oil in heavy 10-inch skillet over low heat. Add garlic and cook until tender, stirring occasionally, about 5 minutes.

Coarsely chop escarole in batches, using 6 to 8 on/off turns. Add to garlic and stir over medium heat until warmed through, about 3 minutes. Mix in ¾ teaspoon salt and pepper. Set escarole mixture aside.

Finely chop mozzarella and Asiago cheeses using on/off turns.

Punch pizza dough down. Cover with towel and let rest 10 minutes.

Roll dough out on floured surface to 18x22-inch rectangle. Transfer dough to prepared pan, pressing gently into sides. Trim off excess dough. Brush bottom and sides of dough with remaining 1 tablespoon oil. Space 16 scant tablespoons escarole evenly over crust; flatten each slightly. Top each with 1½ teaspoons ricotta, smoothing slightly. Fill in spaces with remaining escarole. Sprinkle mozzarella and Asiago evenly over pizza. Bake until bottom of crust is golden, 18 to 20 minutes. Serve immediately.

*Whole Wheat Pizza Dough

After the dough has risen, it can be rolled out and baked immediately or refrigerated or frozen.

Makes about 1½ pounds dough

1 envelope dry yeast
1 cup plus 3 tablespoons warm water (105°F to 115°F)
1 teaspoon honey

1¼ cups (or more) bread flour
1¼ cups whole wheat flour
4½ teaspoons olive oil
1 teaspoon salt

Sprinkle yeast over warm water in bowl; add honey and stir to blend. Let stand until foamy, about 5 minutes.

Combine 1¼ cups bread flour, whole wheat flour, oil and salt in processor. With machine running, add yeast mixture through feed tube and process 20 seconds. If dough sticks to bowl, add more bread flour through feed tube 1 tablespoon at a time, incorporating each addition before adding next. If dough is dry, add water through feed tube 1 teaspoon at a time, incorporating each addition before adding next. Process until smooth and elastic, about 40 seconds. (If machine slows, divide dough in half and process each piece 40 seconds.)

Transfer dough to oiled bowl, turning to coat entire surface. Cover bowl with oiled plastic. Let dough rise in warm draft-free area until doubled in volume, about 1 hour. *(Can be prepared 3 days ahead and refrigerated or 2 months ahead and frozen. Thaw frozen dough in refrigerator 6 to 8 hours.)*

Potato-crusted Pizza

Makes one 12-inch pizza

Crust
- 1 pound boiling potatoes, peeled and coarsely chopped
- 1½ ounces Romano cheese, grated (⅓ cup)
- 1½ ounces mozzarella cheese (preferably low moisture), grated (⅓ cup)
- ½ teaspoon coarse salt
- ⅓ cup plus 1 tablespoon milk
- 2 eggs, separated, room temperature
- ⅔ cup all purpose flour

Topping
- 2 tablespoons olive oil
- 1 large garlic clove, minced
- Pinch of dried red pepper flakes
- 2 ounces mushrooms, thinly sliced (1 cup)
- 2 teaspoons fresh lemon juice
- 4½ teaspoons minced fresh parsley
- 1 medium tomato, seeded and diced (½ cup)
- 2 ounces mozzarella cheese, grated (½ cup)
- 1½ ounces provolone cheese, grated (⅓ cup)
- 3 tablespoons grated Romano or Parmesan cheese
- 2 tablespoons chopped prosciutto
  Olive oil
  Salt and freshly ground pepper

For crust: Cook potatoes in boiling salted water until very tender. Drain. Puree through food mill or sieve into medium bowl (about 1⅓ cups). *Do not use processor.*

Preheat oven to 400°F. Generously oil 12-inch cast-iron skillet or metal pizza pan. Mix cheeses and ¼ teaspoon salt into potato puree. Beat milk and yolks to blend in another bowl. Using wooden spoon, stir into potato mixture alternating with flour. Beat whites with remaining salt until stiff but not dry. Gently fold into potato mixture; dough will be sticky. Spread into prepared pan. Bake until lightly browned and tester inserted in center comes out clean, 25 to 30 minutes. Pierce entire surface of crust gently with fork.

For topping: Preheat broiler. Heat oil in heavy medium skillet over high heat. Add garlic and red pepper flakes and stir 30 seconds. Add mushrooms and stir 1½ minutes. Blend in lemon juice. Remove from heat. Stir in 3 teaspoons parsley. Spread mushroom mixture over crust. Top with tomato. Sprinkle with mozzarella, provolone, 2½ tablespoons Romano and prosciutto. Drizzle lightly with olive oil. Season with salt and pepper. Broil 6 inches from heat source until edges are well browned and cheese is bubbly, watching carefully, 1 to 2 minutes. Sprinkle with remaining parsley and Romano. Cut into wedges and serve.

3 ❦ *Meat*

It is no surprise that this is one of the biggest chapters in the book. Whether quick-cooked and served with a fresh light sauce, marinated and grilled, or braised in a flavorful gravy with plenty of fresh vegetables, meat—beef, veal, lamb and pork—is still the number-one choice for a satisfying meal.

These main dishes can be prepared with little effort and cover a range of possibilities, from casual family suppers to an important dinner party. There's an easy One-hour Mixed Grill Couscous (page 42), really a meal-in-one, with vegetables and fluffy couscous arranged with assorted grilled meats; Southwestern Beef and Vegetable Stew (page 53), great to make ahead; Country-style Pork Ribs and Sauerkraut (page 70), a hearty microwave dish; and Polenta and Sausage Casserole (page 73), inspired by Italian country cooking.

For almost effortless entertaining, nothing is as impressive as an elegant meat dish. Try the succulent Paniolo New York Strip Roast (page 46), simply coated with mustard and coarse salt and roasted in the oven; Curried Lamb Shanks (page 63), redolent of spices and served with a rice and pine nut pilaf; Veal Paillards with Chive Cream Sauce (page 57), quickly sautéed cutlets in a rich cream sauce; and Roast Loin of Pork in Lemon-Garlic Marinade (page 65), fragrant with citrus and spices.

Beef

One-hour Mixed Grill Couscous

6 to 8 servings

3 tablespoons bacon fat
2 large onions, coarsely chopped
3 celery stalks, sliced ¼ inch thick on diagonal (leaves reserved)
3 10¾-ounce cans chicken broth
1 15½-ounce can garbanzo beans (chick-peas), drained
1 15-ounce can lima beans (with liquid)
1 7-ounce bottle pilsner beer
3 carrots, sliced ¼ inch thick on diagonal
¼ pound mushrooms, thinly sliced
1 2-ounce jar chopped pimientos, drained

2 large garlic cloves, minced
2 tablespoons soy sauce
3 bay leaves
1 teaspoon sugar
1 teaspoon poultry seasoning
½ teaspoon freshly ground white pepper

1 1-pound box couscous, cooked according to package directions
3¼ pounds assorted grilled or broiled meats (such as flank steak, filet mignon, kielbasa, lamb chops, pork chops)

Melt bacon fat in Dutch oven over low heat. Add onions and celery and sauté until lightly browned. Add next 13 ingredients. Cover pot and cook vegetables 30 minutes.

Mound couscous in center of large platter. Arrange grilled meats around couscous. Ladle vegetables and broth over. Garnish with celery leaves. Serve immediately.

Beef Burritos with Creamed Peppers

2 servings; can be doubled or tripled

8 ounces skirt or flank steak
1 large garlic clove, crushed
¼ teaspoon ground cumin
1½ teaspoons olive oil
1½ teaspoons fresh lime juice

1 tablespoon olive oil
1 large onion, thinly sliced
2 Anaheim chilies, roasted, peeled, seeded and cut into thin strips*
1 7-ounce jar roasted red peppers, drained and cut into thin strips

½ cup whipping cream
¾ cup grated Monterey Jack cheese
½ teaspoon dried oregano, crumbled
Salt and freshly ground pepper

1 tablespoon olive oil

4 8-inch flour tortillas
½ cup grated Monterey Jack cheese

Preheat oven to 450°F. Grease 9-inch square baking pan. Rub both sides of steak with garlic and cumin, then with 1½ teaspoons oil and lime juice. Set aside.

Heat 1 tablespoon oil in heavy medium skillet over medium-high heat. Add onion and cook until beginning to brown, stirring frequently, about 6 minutes. Add chilies and peppers and stir until heated through. Add cream, then ¾ cup cheese and stir until mixture thickens, about 1 minute. Add oregano. Season with salt and pepper.

Heat 1 tablespoon oil in heavy large skillet over high heat. Season steak with salt and pepper. Cook until brown, about 1½ minutes per side for very rare. Transfer meat to work surface. Halve across width, then cut against grain into thin slices.

Hold tortilla over gas burner on low or place on electric burner on low until heated through, about 15 seconds per side. Place on work surface. Spoon ¼ cup pepper mixture down center. Top with ¼ of meat. Roll up tortilla, enclosing filling. Arrange in baking pan seam side down. Repeat with remaining tortillas, ¾ cup pepper mixture and remaining meat. Spoon remaining pepper mixture over tortillas. Sprinkle with ½ cup cheese. *(Can be assembled 2 hours ahead. Cover with foil and refrigerate.)* Bake uncovered (covered if burritos were refrigerated) until cheese melts, 5 to 10 minutes. Serve immediately.

*Canned whole mild green chilies can be substituted; do not roast.

Orange Beef with Snow Peas and Water Chestnuts

Rice makes a nice accompaniment for soaking up the zesty sauce.

4 servings

½ pound flank steak, trimmed

⅓ cup orange peel julienne
3 green onions, minced
3 tablespoons soy sauce
2 tablespoons oriental sesame oil
1 tablespoon mirin* (syrupy rice wine)
1 tablespoon minced peeled fresh ginger
1 large garlic clove, minced
1 teaspoon sugar
¼ teaspoon dried red pepper flakes

2 medium carrots, peeled and cut into matchstick julienne
1 cup thinly sliced water chestnuts (preferably fresh)
½ pound snow peas, strings removed
2 tablespoons beef broth or water
3 green onions, cut into matchstick julienne
1 teaspoon hot chili oil*

Wrap steak tightly in plastic and freeze until firm but not solid.

Cut steak across grain into ¼-inch-thick slices. Cut each slice lengthwise into ¼-inch-wide strips. Place in large bowl. Mix in orange peel, minced green onions, soy sauce, 1 tablespoon sesame oil, mirin, ginger, garlic, sugar and dried pepper flakes. Marinate 45 minutes, mixing occasionally.

Heat remaining 1 tablespoon sesame oil in heavy large skillet over high heat. Add carrots, water chestnuts and snow peas and stir-fry 2 minutes. Add broth. Reduce heat to low, cover and steam 2 minutes. Mix in green onion julienne. Transfer vegetables to large bowl using slotted spoon. Add chili oil to skillet. Increase heat to high and cook 1 minute. Add steak with marinade. Stir-fry until most juices have evaporated but meat is still rare, about 2 minutes. Return vegetables to skillet and stir until heated through, about 1 minute. Serve immediately.

*Available at oriental markets.

Marinated Sesame Beef

2 to 4 servings

1½ cups chopped green onions
1 cup soy sauce
1 cup water
½ cup sugar
¼ cup sesame seeds
6 garlic cloves, minced

1 teaspoon freshly ground pepper
1 pound bottom round of beef, thinly sliced

Freshly cooked rice
Chopped green onions

Combine first 7 ingredients in bowl. Place beef in ovenproof glass baking dish. Pour marinade over. Cover and refrigerate overnight, stirring occasionally.

Prepare barbecue (medium-high heat) or preheat broiler. Drain marinade from meat. Grill beef to desired doneness, turning once, about 8 minutes for medium-rare. Mound rice on platter. Top with meat. Garnish with chopped green onions.

Beef Paillards with Asparagus and Red Wine Sauce

4 servings

4 6-ounce ⅓-inch-thick boned rib eye steaks

16 asparagus tips

Salt and freshly ground pepper
2 tablespoons vegetable oil

¾ cup dry red wine
1 shallot, minced
¼ teaspoon dried thyme, crumbled
½ bay leaf

Quick Brown Sauce*
2 tablespoons (¼ stick) well-chilled unsalted butter, cut into 2 pieces
2 teaspoons snipped fresh chives
2 teaspoons minced fresh parsley
1½ teaspoons minced fresh tarragon or ½ teaspoon dried, crumbled
Pinch of sugar (optional)

1 tablespoon butter

Pound each steak between 2 sheets of plastic wrap to thickness of ¼ inch, using flat meat pounder or rolling pin. *(Can be prepared 4 hours ahead. Cover tightly and refrigerate. Bring to room temperature before continuing.)*

Preheat oven to 275°F. Blanch asparagus in saucepan of boiling salted water until crisp-tender, about 2 minutes. Rinse under cold water and drain.

Sprinkle steaks with salt and pepper. Heat oil in heavy large skillet over high heat. Add half of steaks to skillet and cook until brown, about 45 seconds per side. Arrange on ovenproof platter, cover and keep warm in oven. Cook remaining steaks.

Discard fat from skillet. Add wine and return to boil, scraping up any browned bits. Add shallot, thyme and bay leaf. Boil until reduced to ¼ cup, stirring occasionally, about 4 minutes.

Strain wine into heavy medium saucepan, pressing on shallot. Whisk in brown sauce. Boil until reduced to saucelike consistency, whisking constantly. Reduce heat to low and whisk in 2 tablespoons butter 1 piece at a time. Remove from heat and stir in chives, parsley and tarragon. Adjust seasoning, adding pinch of sugar if sauce is too tart. Discard bay leaf.

Melt 1 tablespoon butter in heavy small skillet over medium heat. Add asparagus and quickly reheat. Spoon sauce over beef. Garnish with asparagus.

*Quick Brown Sauce

Makes about 1 cup

1 tablespoon vegetable oil
½ large onion, diced
½ medium carrot, diced
1¾ cups rich beef stock (preferably homemade)
5 parsley stems

1 bay leaf
¼ teaspoon dried thyme, crumbled

2 teaspoons potato starch or arrowroot dissolved in 4 teaspoons cold water

Heat oil in heavy medium saucepan over medium-high heat. Add onion and carrot and cook until well browned, stirring frequently, about 8 minutes. Mix in stock, parsley, bay leaf and thyme. Bring to boil, reduce heat and simmer 30 minutes.

Strain stock into bowl, pressing on vegetables to extract all liquid. Set in larger bowl of cold water and let stand 10 minutes. Skim off fat. Rinse saucepan. Measure stock and return to saucepan. If necessary, boil until reduced to 1 cup. Reduce heat to medium. Gradually whisk in potato starch. Boil until thickened, whisking constantly, about 1 minute. *(Can be prepared 2 days ahead and refrigerated. Cover top of warm sauce with pieces of butter to prevent skin from forming.)*

Beef Paillards with Shiitake Mushrooms and Madeira

4 servings

4 6-ounce ⅓-inch-thick boned rib eye steaks

¼ pound fresh shiitake mushrooms, rinsed, halved and thinly sliced
4 tablespoons (½ stick) unsalted butter
2 tablespoons vegetable oil

1 large shallot, minced
Salt and freshly ground pepper
¼ pound mushrooms, halved and thinly sliced
⅓ cup Madeira

1 tablespoon minced fresh parsley

Pound each steak between 2 sheets of plastic wrap to thickness of ¼ inch, using flat meat pounder or rolling pin. *(Can be prepared 4 hours ahead. Cover tightly and refrigerate. Bring to room temperature before continuing.)*

Preheat oven to 275°F. Pat shiitake dry. Melt 2 tablespoons butter with 1 tablespoon oil in heavy large skillet over medium heat. Stir in shiitake, shallot, salt and pepper. Cook until shiitake are just tender, stirring frequently, about 4 minutes. Transfer to plate using slotted spoon. Add remaining 2 tablespoons butter to pan and melt over medium-high heat. Add mushrooms, salt and pepper. Cook until light brown, stirring frequently, about 3 minutes. Return shiitake to skillet and reheat until sizzling. Add Madeira, reduce heat to medium and stir until all liquid is absorbed, about 3 minutes. Adjust seasoning. Remove mushroom mixture from heat.

Heat ridged grill pan or heavy large skillet over high heat until tip of steak sizzles when touched to grill. Pat steaks dry, sprinkle with salt and pepper and brush with some of remaining oil. Cook 1 or 2 steaks (do not crowd) 30 seconds on first side. Brush with oil and turn. Cook 30 seconds longer for rare meat, pressing against ridges with spatula if curling. Transfer steaks to ovenproof platter, cover and keep warm in oven while grilling remaining steaks. Reheat mushroom mixture. Add parsley and spoon over steaks. Serve paillards immediately.

Steaks with Zesty Tarragon Butter

6 servings

2 medium shallots
2 tablespoons chopped fresh parsley
4 teaspoons tarragon vinegar
½ teaspoon dried tarragon, crumbled
½ teaspoon freshly ground pepper

½ cup (1 stick) butter, well chilled, cut into small pieces

6 beef tenderloin steaks

Combine shallots, parsley, vinegar, tarragon and pepper in processor and mince using several on/off turns. Add butter and blend well. Transfer to waxed paper and form into cylinder. Refrigerate or freeze until firm.

Grill, broil or pan-fry steaks to desired doneness. Transfer to individual plates. Slice butter evenly into 6 rounds (or thinner if desired). Set atop steaks and serve.

Portuguese Steak

2 servings

1 tablespoon red wine vinegar
1 garlic clove, minced

2 8-ounce beef tenderloin steaks (about 1 inch thick)
Salt and freshly ground pepper

1 tablespoon butter
1 tablespoon olive oil

½ cup dry red wine
1½ teaspoons tomato paste
2 tablespoons (¼ stick) butter, cut into pieces, room temperature
2 thin slices presunto* or prosciutto, chopped
2 tablespoons minced fresh parsley

Combine vinegar and garlic in nonaluminum bowl. Let stand 10 minutes.

Pat steaks dry. Sprinkle lightly with salt and pepper on both sides. Rub vinegar mixture into steaks on both sides. Let stand at room temperature 10 minutes; or cover with plastic wrap and refrigerate for up to 1 hour.

Melt 1 tablespoon butter with oil in heavy medium skillet over medium heat. Add steaks and cook to desired doneness, about 4 minutes per side for rare. Transfer steaks to plates and cover with foil. Pour off fat in skillet. Stir in wine over high heat, scraping up any browned bits. Boil until liquid is syrupy, about 3 minutes. Whisk in tomato paste. Remove from heat. Whisk in remaining 2 tablespoons butter 1 piece at a time, incorporating each piece completely before adding next. Stir in presunto and parsley. Spoon sauce over steaks and serve.

*Available at specialty meat markets.

Paniolo New York Strip Roast

This simple method for cooking a roast depends on an accurate oven. Be sure to order this cut, also known as a top loin roast, several days in advance.

12 servings

1 10-pound New York strip loin roast, room temperature
1¼ cups Dijon mustard
1 pound coarse salt

Sautéed Mushrooms*
Fresh parsley sprigs

Pat meat dry. Coat with mustard. Press salt into mustard to coat completely. Place meat on rack in roasting pan. Let stand while preheating oven.

Preheat gas oven to 375°F or electric oven to 350°F for 1 hour. Place roast in oven. Reduce gas oven to 350°F. Cook roast 1 hour; *do not open oven.* Turn oven off and let roast stand 1 hour; *do not open oven.*

Remove roast from oven and let stand 15 minutes. Dust off loose salt. Slice beef thickly and divide among plates. Spoon Sautéed Mushrooms alongside. Garnish with parsley sprigs and serve.

*Sautéed Mushrooms

12 servings

½ cup (1 stick) butter
½ cup minced shallots
3 pounds mushrooms, sliced

Salt and freshly ground pepper
2 tablespoons Madeira
Minced fresh parsley

Melt butter in heavy large skillet over medium heat. Add shallots and cook until softened, stirring frequently, about 5 minutes. Increase heat to high. Add mushrooms and season with salt and pepper. Stir until juices evaporate, about 5 minutes. Transfer to bowl. Add Madeira to skillet and bring to boil, scraping up any browned bits. Mix into mushrooms. Stir in parsley.

Polynesian Flank Steak

Accompany with a composed salad of white rice, fresh green peas and mint.

4 to 6 servings

2 tablespoons (¼ stick) butter
1 bunch green onions, finely minced
1 cup dry breadcrumbs
1 papaya, peeled, seeded and coarsely chopped
1 banana, mashed
½ cup unsalted peanuts, coarsely chopped
2 teaspoons soy sauce

1 teaspoon fresh lemon juice
½ teaspoon dried tarragon, crumbled
1 2- to 2½-pound (about) flank steak, well dried, fat trimmed

¾ cup papaya nectar
¼ cup dry white wine
Safflower oil

Melt butter in large skillet over medium-high heat. Add green onion and sauté until soft but not brown. Stir in breadcrumbs, papaya, banana, peanuts, soy sauce, lemon juice and tarragon. Remove from heat. Score meat lightly on both sides. Spread stuffing evenly over meat. Roll up jelly roll style, securing with string several times crosswise and lengthwise.

Preheat oven to 300°F. Combine papaya nectar and wine. Heat oil in large flameproof casserole or Dutch oven over medium-high heat. Add meat and brown on all sides. Pour nectar-wine mixture over. Cover tightly, transfer to oven and roast until tender, about 1 hour, turning occasionally. Transfer to heated platter and let stand 15 minutes. Slice into serving pieces. Spoon small amount of sauce over and serve. Pass remaining sauce separately.

Bacon-stuffed Flank Steak

4 servings

1½ pounds flank steak, trimmed and pounded evenly to ½-inch thickness
1 teaspoon garlic salt

Freshly ground pepper
10 slices bacon, cooked
2 tablespoons chopped fresh parsley
Hollandaise sauce (optional)

Preheat broiler or prepare barbecue grill. Season steak with garlic salt and pepper. Score steak diagonally twice, reversing direction second time to make crisscross pattern. Place bacon lengthwise on steak. Sprinkle parsley over steak. Roll meat lengthwise, securing with toothpicks at 1-inch intervals. Broil or grill, turning frequently, until browned on all sides, about 20 minutes for medium rare. Remove toothpicks. Cut meat into eight 1-inch slices using serrated knife. Serve hot with hollandaise.

Instant Entertaining

Delicious entrées in minutes is our translation of the cooking method called *blanc* or *minute,* in which specially prepared meats or fish are arranged and quick-cooked on the serving plate, then accompanied with sauces and herbs. The basic steps are simple and few; the results are elegant and sublime.

- Thinly slice and divide the meat or fish into serving-size portions.
- Brush ovenproof dinner plates with oil and sprinkle lightly with salt and freshly ground pepper.
- Place a portion of meat or fish in the center of each plate. Brush with oil and season with salt and pepper.
- Baked according to desired doneness and serve directly from the oven with accompanying sauces.

Advance preparation is obviously the key here. Preslicing the meat or fish into the appropriate size frees you from the kitchen until just about 5 minutes before you bring the plates to the table. Here are some good general guidelines for slicing:

- *Small fish fillets,* such as flounder, red snapper, scrod or sole, 4 to 6 ounces each. Remove small bones with tweezers. Cut fillets on the diagonal, trimming each piece neatly to about 4½ by 2 inches. Two fillets will yield two main-course servings.
- *Large, skinless fish fillets* of more than 8 ounces each, such as bluefish, cod, haddock, halibut, salmon, striped bass. Allow ¾ to 1 pound for two main-course servings. Cut as per above or, if fillet is no more than ⅜ inch thick, place on cutting board and slice with knife perpendicular to board. Each piece should be about 4½ by ⅜ inches and weigh 1 ounce. Allow 6 slices (6 ounces) per serving. Press slices together so they appear to be one neat piece before arranging on serving plate.

Flank Steak with Fresh Tomato Sauce

2 to 3 servings

½ to ¾ pound flank steak, trimmed

Marinade
- ⅓ cup olive oil
- 1½ tablespoons fresh lemon juice
- ½ teaspoon minced garlic
- ½ teaspoon coarse salt
- 2 drops hot pepper sauce
  Freshly ground pepper

Sauce
- 1½ pounds ripe tomatoes (preferably Italian plum), peeled, seeded and finely chopped
- ¾ teaspoon coarse salt
- 2 tablespoons chopped fresh herbs (tarragon, basil, mint, parsley or combination)
  Salt and freshly ground pepper

Slice flank steak according to instructions above. Arrange in single layer in shallow pan or baking dish.

- *Tail-end fish fillet with skin,* such as bluefish, halibut or salmon: If it contains a center bone, remove it so there are two fillets. Discard bone and carefully remove any small bones with tweezers. Place fillet skin side down on cutting board. Cut fish into ¼-inch slices with flexible long knife parallel to the board. Keep slicing until only skin remains to be discarded. (Allow 4 to 5 ounces per main-course serving.) If the slices are uneven, press them together to hide ragged edges and make them appear to be one slice.

- *Chicken breasts:* Remove skin and bones and cut down center in two halves. Remove white tendon on underside of each half. Press breast down and butterfly by slicing in half horizontally using a long thin knife placed parallel to the board, stopping just before you cut all the way through. Open up as you would a book. With your fingers, press to flatten into a neat, thin piece. Repeat with remaining chicken breasts.

- *Veal scallops:* Allow 3 scallops, 3½ to 4 ounces, per main-course serving. Place veal scallop between waxed paper and pound to an even thickness, about ¹⁄₁₆ inch.

- *Flank steak:* Cut steak into strips about ⅛ to ¼ inch thick across grain, holding sharp knife at an angle. Allow 6 slices or about 3½ to 4 ounces per main-course serving.

This method of cooking is ideal for the busy cook who likes to entertain. Slicing the meat or fish and dividing it into serving portions can all be done several hours in advance. If there's room in the refrigerator, place the portions on prepared dinner plates and cover. Or separate each portion with waxed paper and stack them in the refrigerator. The sauces can be partially cooked ahead of time to be finished while the plates are in the oven. Just remember to start with plates, fish or meat and sauce at room temperature. And, because food is cooked directly on the dinner plates, check to make certain yours are ovenproof.

For marinade: Combine all ingredients for marinade in small bowl and blend well. Pour 2½ tablespoons over meat (reserve remainder). Turn slices to coat both sides. Let stand at least 30 minutes, or refrigerate overnight.

For sauce: Place tomatoes in strainer. Stir in salt and let tomatoes drain at least 30 minutes, shaking strainer occasionally. Transfer tomatoes to saucepan, add remaining marinade and 1½ tablespoons herbs. Season with salt and freshly ground pepper. Warm sauce over low heat.

Preheat oven to 450°F. Sprinkle ovenproof plates lightly with salt and pepper. Press meat lightly to remove excess marinade. Arrange meat in center of plates, leaving about ¾ inch between each slice. Sprinkle lightly with salt and pepper. Bake 2½ to 3 minutes. Remove plates from oven. Spoon about ⅓ cup heated sauce around each serving. Sprinkle with remaining herbs. Serve immediately.

Tournedos en Champagne

4 servings

¾ cup (1½ sticks) unsalted butter
½ cup diced onion
1 large garlic clove, minced
1¼ cups Champagne
  Bouquet garni (1 bay leaf, 1 fresh thyme sprig or ¼ teaspoon dried, 1 parsley sprig)

2 large garlic cloves
4 6-ounce beef tenderloin fillets
  Freshly ground pepper
2 tablespoons duxelles* (optional)
1 cup whipping cream
  Salt and freshly ground pepper

Melt 2 tablespoons butter in heavy medium skillet over medium heat. Add onion and minced garlic and brown lightly, about 5 to 6 minutes. Add 1 cup Champagne and bouquet garni, increase heat to medium-high and cook until liquid is reduced to ¼ cup, about 5 minutes. Remove from heat; discard bouquet garni.

Melt remaining butter in heavy large skillet over medium-high heat. Add whole garlic cloves. Sprinkle fillets with pepper and add to sizzling butter. Cook until browned, turning once, about 3 minutes per side for rare. Transfer fillets to heated platter. Reduce heat to medium. Add duxelles and remaining Champagne to skillet and deglaze, scraping up any browned bits. Increase heat to medium-high and continue cooking until syrupy, about 4 minutes. Discard garlic cloves. Stir in cream. Cook until reduced by half, about 5 to 7 minutes. Season sauce with salt and pepper.

Rewarm onion mixture over low heat. Top each fillet with some of onion mixture. Spoon sauce over and serve.

*Finely minced mushrooms cooked until liquid evaporates.

Pepper Steak

4 servings

1 3½-pound sirloin steak (1½ inches thick), edges scored at 2-inch intervals
2 tablespoons coarsely ground pepper
1 teaspoon salt

1 tablespoon butter
1 tablespoon olive oil

½ cup dry white wine
¼ cup whipping cream
¼ cup brandy

Rub both sides of steak with pepper. Sprinkle with salt. Melt butter with oil in heavy large skillet over high heat. Add steak and sear on both sides. Reduce heat to medium-high. Cook 6 to 7 minutes on each side for rare. Transfer steak to serving platter.

Add wine to pan and bring to boil, scraping up any browned bits. Add cream and boil sauce until reduced by half. Pour brandy into pan and heat briefly; ignite with match. When flames subside, pour sauce over steak. Serve immediately.

Savory Chateaubriand

6 servings

1 2- to 3-pound chateaubriand
1 tablespoon Worcestershire sauce
1 tablespoon wine vinegar
1 tablespoon catsup

  Pinch of onion powder
  Pinch of garlic powder
  Salt and freshly ground pepper

Arrange meat in baking dish. Combine all remaining ingredients in small bowl. Pour over meat and marinate 1 hour.

Preheat oven to 450°F. Roast meat to desired doneness. Serve immediately.

Garlic-roasted Chateaubriand with Cognac-Mustard Sauce

8 servings

2 2- to 2½-pound beef tenderloins, trimmed
4 medium garlic cloves, finely slivered
3 tablespoons olive oil

Sauce
1 tablespoon unsalted butter
4 medium shallots, minced

2 cups beef stock, preferably homemade
2 tablespoons Cognac
2 tablespoons Dijon mustard
3 tablespoons minced fresh parsley
½ cup (1 stick) unsalted butter, cut into 8 pieces
Salt and freshly ground pepper

Preheat oven to 450°F. Cut ¾-inch-deep slits in meat. Insert garlic slivers into slits. Brush meat with 2 tablespoons oil. Heat remaining oil in heavy large skillet over medium-high heat. Add meat and brown on all sides. Do not wash skillet. Set meat on rack in roasting pan. Roast to desired doneness, about 30 minutes for rare.

For sauce: Melt 1 tablespoon butter in same skillet. Add shallots and cook until softened, about 5 minutes.

Pour off fat from roasting pan. Set pan over high heat. Stir in stock, scraping up browned bits. Add stock to shallots. Boil until reduced by half. Add Cognac and boil 1 minute. Reduce heat to low. Whisk in mustard. Stir in parsley. Whisk in butter 1 piece at a time. Season with salt and pepper.

Cut meat into ½-inch slices. Arrange slices on individual plates. Spoon sauce over. Serve immediately.

Wine- and Herb-braised Pot Roast

8 servings

1 4-inch-square piece salt pork, cut into ½-inch pieces

2 tablespoons olive oil
2 medium onions, sliced
4 garlic cloves, minced

1 4- to 6-pound boneless chuck, round roast or brisket
Salt and freshly ground pepper
2 pounds canned peeled Italian plum tomatoes (undrained)
2 cups dry red wine

3 parsley sprigs
1 bay leaf
1 tablespoon orange peel julienne
½ teaspoon dried thyme, crumbled
½ teaspoon dried marjoram, crumbled
½ teaspoon dried basil, crumbled

3 tablespoons cold water
1½ tablespoons all purpose flour
Minced fresh parsley

Blanch salt pork in boiling water 5 minutes. Drain well; set aside.

Heat oil in Dutch oven or deep heavy large skillet over medium heat. Add onions, salt pork and garlic and sauté until pork is browned, 20 minutes.

Remove onions and pork with slotted spoon; set aside. Increase heat to medium-high. Pat beef dry; season with salt and pepper. Add to Dutch oven and brown on both sides, about 20 minutes. Return onions and pork to pan. Add tomatoes with liquid, wine, parsley sprigs, bay leaf, orange peel, thyme, marjoram and basil. Reduce heat to low, cover and simmer until beef is tender, 3½ to 4 hours.

Remove meat from pan; keep warm. Degrease sauce. Mix water and flour; stir half into sauce. Bring to boil. Reduce heat and simmer until thickened, adding remaining flour mixture if desired. Slice meat. Arrange on platter; pour sauce over. Garnish with parsley.

Apple Sauerkraut Roast

6 servings

1 large tart apple, cored and sliced
1 3-pound lean boneless beef roast
1 27-ounce can sauerkraut, rinsed and drained
1 16-ounce can chopped tomatoes, drained
¼ cup firmly packed brown sugar
Salt and freshly ground pepper

1 ⅞-ounce package dry onion gravy mix
Freshly cooked mashed potatoes
Chopped fresh parsley (optional garnish)

Arrange apple slices in bottom of slow cooker. Position roast over apples, cutting meat in half to fit, if necessary. Add sauerkraut, tomatoes, brown sugar, salt and pepper. Cover and cook on Low until meat is tender, about 8 hours.

Stir in gravy mix. Cover and cook until heated through, about 15 minutes. Serve hot over mashed potatoes. Top each serving with parsley, if desired.

Korean-style Short Ribs

During barbecue season, cook these ribs on the grill.

4 servings

1 cup soy sauce
½ cup oriental sesame oil
6 large garlic cloves, minced
¼ cup chopped green onions
¼ cup sugar

2 teaspoons sesame seeds
½ teaspoon distilled white vinegar
½ teaspoon dry mustard
½ teaspoon freshly ground pepper
8 large beef short ribs

Combine first 9 ingredients in medium bowl. Trim excess fat from ribs. Score at ½-inch intervals almost to bone. Place ribs in glass baking dish. Pour marinade over. Cover and refrigerate overnight, turning occasionally.

Preheat broiler. Transfer ribs to broiler rack, draining marinade. Broil about 3 inches from heat until charred, about 8 minutes per side. Serve immediately.

Mustard-glazed Corned Beef Brisket

6 servings

1 4- to 5-pound corned beef brisket

8 whole black peppercorns
2 bay leaves

½ cup Dijon mustard
1 teaspoon dry mustard

½ cup honey
⅓ cup Sherry wine vinegar
⅓ cup firmly packed light brown sugar
1 tablespoon oriental sesame oil

Place brisket in large pot. Add enough water to cover. Cover pot. Refrigerate brisket at least 6 hours or overnight.

Drain brisket. Add water to cover, peppercorns and bay leaves. Bring to boil. Reduce heat, cover and simmer until tender, about 3½ hours. Drain brisket. Cool. Cover and chill overnight.

Transfer brisket to shallow roasting pan, fat side up. Bring to room temperature. Preheat oven to 350°F. Whisk mustards in heavy small saucepan. Stir in remaining ingredients. Simmer 5 minutes, stirring constantly. Spread glaze evenly over top of brisket. Bake until heated through, about 45 minutes.

Burgundy Beef Stroganoff

6 servings

¼ cup all purpose flour
1 teaspoon salt
1 teaspoon dried thyme, crumbled
½ teaspoon freshly ground pepper
2 pounds round steak, cut into
   1½x¼-inch strips
½ cup (1 stick) butter
1 medium onion, finely chopped
1 cup beef broth
1 cup Burgundy

2 tablespoons (¼ stick) butter
½ pound mushrooms, sliced

2 cups sour cream
3 tablespoons tomato paste
1 tablespoon Worcestershire sauce
   Freshly cooked rice
   Chopped fresh parsley

Combine flour, salt, thyme and pepper in plastic bag. Add meat and shake to coat well. Remove meat, shaking off excess flour. Melt ½ cup butter in large skillet over medium heat. Add meat and brown lightly, about 3 minutes. Add onion and stir until tender, about 3 minutes. Pour in broth and wine. Simmer mixture until meat is tender, 30 to 45 minutes.

Melt 2 tablespoons butter in small skillet over medium heat. Add mushrooms and sauté until just tender, 3 to 4 minutes. Stir mushrooms into meat.

Blend sour cream, tomato paste and Worcestershire sauce in small bowl. Slowly stir into meat mixture and heat; do not boil. Mound rice on serving dish. Spoon meat over. Top with parsley.

Southwestern Beef and Vegetable Stew

Makes about 8 cups

3 tablespoons olive oil
1 pound chuck or other beef stew
   meat, cut into ¾-inch cubes
1 medium onion, chopped
3 garlic cloves, minced
1 28-ounce can tomatoes, chopped
   (liquid reserved)
½ pound mushrooms, sliced
4 celery stalks, sliced
3 medium carrots, peeled and sliced

1 medium red bell pepper, seeded and
   cut julienne
1 medium zucchini, sliced
½ cup minced fresh parsley
1 dried red chili
1 teaspoon dried basil, crumbled
½ teaspoon dried oregano, crumbled
½ teaspoon dried sage, crumbled
   Salt and freshly ground pepper

Heat oil in heavy large saucepan or Dutch oven over medium-high heat. Add beef, onion and garlic and cook until meat is browned, stirring frequently, about 8 minutes. Mix in remaining ingredients. Reduce heat to low, cover and simmer 3 hours, stirring occasionally. Cool to room temperature. Cover and refrigerate at least 6 hours or overnight. Serve stew hot.

Beef and Olive Stew

4 to 6 servings

2 tablespoons vegetable oil
1 large onion, chopped
2 garlic cloves, minced
2 pounds flank steak, cut into
¼x2-inch strips
1 15-ounce can tomato sauce
2 tablespoons red wine vinegar
1 tablespoon dried oregano,
crumbled

Freshly ground pepper
½ cup pimiento-stuffed green olives,
sliced
1 to 2 marinated jalapeño chilies,
diced
Freshly cooked rice

Heat oil in large skillet over medium heat. Add onion and garlic and stir until translucent, about 6 minutes. Increase heat to medium-high. Add steak and stir until browned, about 3 minutes. Blend in tomato sauce, vinegar, oregano and pepper. Simmer until meat is tender and sauce is thickened, 30 to 40 minutes. Add olives and chilies and stir until heated through. Spoon over rice. Serve immediately.

Beef Carbonnade with Fresh Ginger

4 servings

6 medium onions
3 tablespoons vegetable oil
1 tablespoon sugar

2½ tablespoons all purpose flour
1¼ cups beer
1 cup beef broth
1 teaspoon dried thyme, crumbled
Bouquet garni (1 sprig parsley,
leafy tops of 2 celery stalks and
1 bay leaf)

1 ½-inch piece fresh ginger, peeled
2¼ pounds boneless beef chuck,
trimmed, sliced ⅓ inch thick and
cut into 2x1-inch pieces
1 teaspoon salt
Freshly ground pepper

1½ tablespoons red wine vinegar
Buttered noodles

Slice onions in processor fitted with medium slicer, using medium pressure. Heat oil in heavy 3-quart saucepan over medium-low heat. Add onions, cover and cook until soft, stirring occasionally, about 15 minutes. Stir in sugar. Increase heat to medium and cook uncovered until onions are golden, stirring frequently, about 30 more minutes.

Add flour and stir 2 minutes. Add beer, broth, thyme and bouquet garni. Simmer until liquid thickens, stirring occasionally, 10 minutes. Set aside.

Position rack in center of oven and then preheat to 350°F.

Insert steel knife. With machine running, drop ginger through feed tube and mince finely. Stir into onion mixture. Season both sides of meat with salt and pepper. Spoon ⅓ of onion mixture into 3-quart baking dish. Add half of meat, then continue layering, ending with onion mixture. Cover and bake until tender, about 2 hours.

Discard bouquet garni. Stir in vinegar. Adjust seasoning. Serve carbonnade immediately with buttered noodles.

Dynamite Chili

2 servings

2 cups water
½ cup dried pinto beans, soaked overnight* and drained

1 tablespoon vegetable oil
1 onion, sliced
½ green pepper, cored, seeded and chopped
1 garlic clove, minced
⅔ pound boneless pork, cut into ½-inch cubes
⅓ pound beef stew meat, cut into ½-inch cubes
1 16-ounce can whole tomatoes, drained

2 tablespoons chili powder
1 diced green chili or 2 tablespoons canned chopped green chilies (or to taste)
1 teaspoon dried oregano, crumbled
2 teaspoons cumin
⅓ cup dry red wine
Salt and freshly ground pepper
2 tablespoons instant tortilla mix, mixed with enough water to form a paste (optional)

Combine water and beans in medium saucepan and bring to boil over medium-high heat. Reduce heat and cook until tender, about 1 hour.

Heat oil in 10-inch skillet over medium-high heat. Add onion, green pepper and garlic and sauté until tender. Transfer to Dutch oven and set aside. Add pork and beef to same skillet and brown well. Stir into vegetables. Add beans and their liquid, tomatoes and seasonings and mix well. Cover and simmer 1 hour. Add wine and cook, uncovered, until thickened, about 30 minutes. Season with salt and pepper. If mixture is too liquid, stir in tortilla paste to thicken.

*Beans can be quick-soaked. Boil 2 minutes in water to cover. Remove from heat, cover and let stand 1 hour. Drain beans thoroughly.

Hangover Hash

4 servings

½ pound coarsely ground round steak
½ pound coarsely ground lamb
½ pound boiling potatoes, peeled and chopped
½ pound Granny Smith apples, cored and diced
¼ pound mushrooms, sliced

¼ cup Calvados
⅛ teaspoon dried thyme, crumbled
Dry mustard (optional)
Salt and freshly ground pepper
2 egg yolks, beaten to blend
4 poached eggs

Brown beef and lamb well in heavy large skillet over high heat. Remove using slotted spoon; set aside. Add potatoes and apples to skillet. Reduce heat to medium, cover and cook 10 minutes. Add mushrooms and continue cooking until potatoes are soft, about 10 minutes. Mix in beef, lamb, Calvados, thyme and mustard (if desired). Season with salt and pepper. Stir in yolks. Increase heat to medium-high and cook 5 minutes, stirring frequently. Spoon hash onto plates. Top with poached eggs and serve.

Twenty-minute Tamale Pie

4 to 6 servings

2 tablespoons (¼ stick) butter
1 pound lean ground beef
1 onion, chopped
1 17-ounce can whole kernel corn, undrained
1 16-ounce can stewed tomatoes, drained
1 cup sour cream
1 cup yellow cornmeal

1 4½-ounce can sliced ripe olives, drained
1 tablespoon chili powder
2 teaspoons salt
½ teaspoon cumin
2 cups shredded Monterey Jack cheese
Green or red chili salsa

Melt butter in large skillet over medium-high heat. Add beef and onion and cook until meat is lightly browned, about 4 to 5 minutes. Drain excess fat. Stir in corn, tomatoes, sour cream, cornmeal, olives, chili powder, salt and cumin and mix thoroughly. Sprinkle cheese over top to within ¼ inch of edge. Cover, reduce heat and simmer 20 minutes. Serve hot with salsa.

Harvest Meat Loaf

Extra applesauce is an excellent accompaniment to this easy dish.

4 to 6 servings

1½ pounds lean ground beef
¾ cup fine dry breadcrumbs
¾ cup applesauce

½ cup catsup
¾ teaspoon salt
Freshly ground pepper

Preheat oven to 350°F. Lightly grease 8-inch square baking pan. Combine ground beef, breadcrumbs, applesauce, catsup, salt and pepper in large bowl and mix lightly but thoroughly. Shape into round or oblong loaf. Transfer to prepared pan. Bake until cooked through, about 1 hour. Serve hot.

Calf's Liver Venetian Style

Serve fried polenta with this classic Italian dish.

4 servings

3 tablespoons butter
3 tablespoons olive oil
2 large onions, thinly sliced
1 pound calf's liver, trimmed and cut into strips

3 tablespoons beef broth
3 tablespoons red wine vinegar
Salt and freshly ground pepper
1 tablespoon minced fresh parsley

Melt butter with oil in heavy large skillet over medium-low heat. Add onions and cook until tender and just golden, stirring occasionally, about 20 minutes; do not brown. Increase heat to high. Add liver and sear quickly on all sides, stirring with wooden spoon, about 5 minutes; do not overcook. Transfer liver and onions to platter. Stir broth and vinegar into skillet, scraping up browned bits; boil briefly. Season with salt and pepper. Pour over liver. Garnish with parsley and serve.

Garlic-scented Mixed Vegetable Sauté
with Pecans and Leek Tart with Cèpes

Irwin Horowitz

Clockwise from left: Fusilli with Zucchini, Plum Tomatoes, Basil and Parsley; Stir-fry of Chicken, Broccoli and Red Bell Pepper; Gingered Shrimp with Asparagus and Green Onions

Orange-glazed Pork Chops

Aromatic Orange Pork Kebabs

Clockwise from right: Flank Steak with Fresh Tomato Sauce; Sea Scallops with Zucchini Mousse; Chicken Breasts with Chinese Mushrooms; Shrimp with Fresh Chives

From top to bottom: Tuna and Green Bean Salad with Yogurt-Dill Dressing; Orange Beef with Snow Peas and Water Chestnuts; Curried Crab, Garden Pea and Papaya Salad in Papaya Shells

Irwin Horowitz

Veal

Lemon Veal with Pink Peppercorns

2 servings

3 garlic cloves, lightly crushed
2 teaspoons pink peppercorns,* lightly crushed
  Juice of 1 large lemon

2 milk-fed veal loin chops (about 7 ounces each), trimmed of all fat
1 tablespoon clarified melted butter

Combine garlic, peppercorns and half of lemon juice in shallow dish. Add veal chops, turning to coat both sides. Refrigerate 1 hour, then let stand at room temperature 30 minutes. Remove from dish using slotted spoon and pat dry. Press some pink peppercorns from dish into each chop.

Heat butter in medium skillet over medium-high heat. Add veal chops and sear on both sides until browned. Discard all but 1 teaspoon fat from skillet. Reduce heat to low, cover and cook chops 10 minutes. Turn and cook until almost firm when pressed, about 8 more minutes. Transfer to heated plates. Add remaining lemon juice to skillet and bring to boil, scraping up any browned bits. Spoon over chops and serve.

*Available in specialty foods stores.

Veal Paillards with Chive Cream Sauce

Veal for paillards is sold under several names: veal cutlets, veal slices, scallops, scaloppine and escalopes.

4 servings

4 4-ounce ⅓-inch-thick veal cutlets
1 small carrot, peeled and quartered lengthwise
1 small zucchini, cut lengthwise into 8 pieces
  Salt

  Freshly ground pepper
4 tablespoons (½ stick) unsalted butter

2 tablespoons vegetable oil
¼ cup all purpose flour
2 medium shallots, minced
½ cup dry white wine
½ cup rich chicken stock (preferably homemade)
1 cup whipping cream
2 tablespoons finely snipped fresh chives

Pound each veal cutlet between 2 sheets of plastic wrap to thickness of ¼ inch, using flat meat pounder or rolling pin. *(Can be prepared 4 hours ahead. Cover tightly and refrigerate. Bring to room temperature before continuing.)*

Cut carrot crosswise into ⅛-inch-thick slices to make dice. Cut zucchini crosswise into ⅛-inch-thick slices. Cover carrots with water in small saucepan. Add pinch of salt. Cover and simmer until tender, about 3½ minutes. Add zucchini, cover and cook until crisp-tender, about 1 minute. Rinse with cold water and drain. *(Can be prepared 1 hour ahead.)*

Preheat oven to 275°F. Sprinkle veal with salt and pepper. Melt 2 tablespoons butter with oil in heavy large skillet over medium-high heat. Dust 2 veal pieces with flour, shaking to remove excess. Add to skillet and cook until light brown, about 1½ minutes per side. Arrange in single layer on ovenproof platter and keep warm in oven.

Repeat with remaining veal.

Discard fat from skillet. Add 1 tablespoon butter and melt over low heat. Add shallots and cook until soft, stirring frequently, about 3 minutes. Pour in wine, increase heat and boil until reduced to ¼ cup, scraping up any browned bits, about 3 minutes. Add stock and boil until reduced to ¼ cup, about 3 minutes. Stir in cream and season with salt and pepper. Simmer over medium heat, until thick enough to coat spoon, stirring frequently, approximately 7 minutes.

Meanwhile, melt remaining 1 tablespoon butter in heavy small skillet over low heat. Add carrot and zucchini and stir until vegetables are just heated through. Season with salt and pepper.

Stir chives into sauce. Adjust seasoning. Transfer veal to plates, discarding any juices accumulated on platter. Spoon sauce over veal; arrange vegetables on each side. Serve immediately.

Sautéed Veal Scallops with Creamy Scrambled Eggs

6 servings

Veal Scallops
- 1 cup all purpose flour
- 1 cup milk
- 2 eggs
- 1 cup dry breadcrumbs
- ¾ cup freshly grated Parmesan cheese
- 1¼ pounds ⅛- to ¼-inch-thick veal scallops, pounded flat
- Salt and freshly ground pepper

- Corn oil

Scrambled Eggs
- 8 eggs
- 3 tablespoons whipping cream
- Salt and freshly ground pepper
- 2 tablespoons (¼ stick) butter

- Basil Tomato Sauce*
- Fresh basil sprigs

For veal: Place flour on large plate. Mix milk and eggs in bowl. Combine breadcrumbs and cheese on another plate. Pat veal dry and sprinkle with salt and pepper. Dredge veal in flour, shaking off excess. Dip in milk, then breadcrumbs, coating well. Let stand at room temperature 15 minutes.

Preheat oven to lowest setting. Lightly coat bottom of heavy large skillet with oil. Heat over medium-high heat. Add veal in batches and cook until golden brown, about 2 minutes per side. Set on platter; keep warm in oven.

For eggs: Whisk eggs, cream, salt and pepper in large bowl to blend. Melt butter in heavy large skillet over medium-low heat. Add egg mixture and stir until eggs are just set but still creamy.

Spoon eggs over veal. Top with Basil Tomato Sauce. Garnish with basil.

*Basil Tomato Sauce

Makes about 4 cups

- ½ cup olive oil
- 1 cup chopped onion
- 1 cup chopped carrot
- 1 28-ounce can Italian plum tomatoes, drained and chopped

- 2 tablespoons minced fresh basil or 2 teaspoons dried, crumbled
- 2 teaspoons minced garlic
- 1 teaspoon salt
- 1 cup whipping cream

Heat oil in heavy large skillet over medium heat. Add onion and carrot. Cook 4 minutes, stirring occasionally. Add all remaining ingredients except cream. Cook until vegetables are very tender and excess liquid evaporates, stirring frequently, about 20 minutes. Puree mixture in blender or processor until smooth. Mix in cream. Adjust seasoning. *(Can be prepared 1 day ahead and refrigerated. Reheat before using.)*

 Lamb

Herb- and Garlic-marinated Leg of Lamb

6 to 8 servings

1 cup olive oil
1 onion, sliced
⅓ cup dry white wine
⅓ cup fresh lemon juice
⅓ cup chopped fresh parsley
3 garlic cloves, minced
1½ tablespoons dried rosemary, crumbled

2 teaspoons Dijon mustard
½ teaspoon salt
½ teaspoon freshly ground pepper
¼ teaspoon dried red pepper flakes
1 5- to 6-pound leg of lamb, boned, butterflied and trimmed

Combine first 11 ingredients. Place lamb in large roasting pan. Pour marinade over. Cover lamb and refrigerate overnight, turning at least once.

Prepare barbecue grill with hot coals. Place lamb on grill and cook 15 minutes per side for rare, basting occasionally with marinade. Remove from heat and let stand 10 minutes before slicing and serving.

Lamb Roast with Pine Nut and Parmesan Crust

6 servings

½ cup pine nuts (2½ ounces), toasted
2 ounces Parmesan cheese (preferably imported), cut into 2 pieces
1 slice of soft white bread (with crust), torn into pieces
2 teaspoons Dijon mustard
1 large garlic clove
½ teaspoon dried rosemary, crumbled

¼ teaspoon salt
Freshly ground pepper
1 egg white

1 3½-pound leg of lamb (sirloin end), boned and trimmed
Salt

Position rack in center of oven and preheat to 450°F. Oil roasting pan.

Insert steel knife in processor. Mix pine nuts, cheese, bread, mustard, garlic, rosemary, ¼ teaspoon salt and pepper. Blend in egg white using 3 to 4 on/off turns.

Season underside of lamb with salt and pepper. Arrange seasoned side down in prepared pan. Using spatula, spread nut mixture over top of lamb, pressing gently to adhere. *(Can be prepared 1 day ahead, covered tightly and refrigerated. Bring to room temperature before continuing.)* Roast lamb 15 minutes. Reduce temperature to 375°F and continue cooking to desired doneness, or about 15 more minutes for rare (thermometer inserted in thickest part of lamb will register 125°F; cook longer for medium rare or well done). Let stand 10 to 15 minutes. Carve lamb into thin slices and serve.

Grilled Lamb Chops with Thyme-Mustard Butter

Mix some of the flavored butter with steamed asparagus for a delicious accompaniment.

2 servings; can be doubled or tripled

Thyme-Mustard Butter
- ¼ cup (½ stick) butter, room temperature
- 1 tablespoon coarse-grained Dijon mustard
- 1 small shallot, minced

- ½ teaspoon fresh lemon juice
- 1½ teaspoons minced fresh thyme or ½ teaspoon dried, crumbled
- Salt and freshly ground pepper

- 4 1¼-inch-thick loin lamb chops

For butter: Blend first 4 ingredients in processor until smooth. Mix in thyme, salt and pepper. *(Can be prepared 3 days ahead, covered and refrigerated. Bring to room temperature before using.)*

Preheat broiler. Spread each lamb chop with ½ teaspoon flavored butter. Broil 2½ minutes. Turn and spread each with ½ teaspoon more butter. Broil about 2½ minutes longer for rare. Transfer to plates. Top each with another ½ teaspoon butter. Serve lamb chops immediately.

Grilled Lamb Chops with Jalapeño Mint Sauce

4 servings

- 8 loin lamb chops
- 4 large garlic cloves, halved
- ½ cup olive oil
- Freshly ground pepper

- 2½ cups veal or beef stock
- ½ cup Champagne vinegar
- ½ cup jalapeño jelly*

- ½ cup mint jelly
- 2 teaspoons minced fresh mint
- 2 teaspoons minced fresh rosemary or ½ teaspoon dried, crumbled

- Whole canned jalapeños, cut into rounds

Pat lamb chops dry. Rub each with cut side of ½ garlic clove. Brush both sides of chops with olive oil. Sprinkle with pepper. Cover and set aside.

Boil stock and vinegar in heavy 2-quart saucepan until reduced to ⅓ cup, about 20 minutes. Whisk in jellies, mint and rosemary.

Meanwhile, prepare barbecue with very hot coals. Grill lamb chops to desired doneness, about 2 minutes per side for medium-rare. Set 2 chops on each plate. Spoon sauce over. Garnish with jalapeño rounds and serve.

*Available at specialty foods stores.

Marinated Lamb Kebabs

6 to 8 servings

- 2 pounds boneless leg of lamb, cut into 1½-inch cubes
- ¾ cup dry white wine
- ½ cup finely chopped onions
- 2 tablespoons olive oil

- 1 tablespoon dried mint, crumbled
- 2 small garlic cloves, minced
- Salt and freshly ground pepper

- Freshly cooked rice

Combine first 6 ingredients in large bowl. Season with salt and pepper. Cover and refrigerate overnight, stirring occasionally.

Prepare barbecue (medium-high heat) or preheat broiler. Thread meat on skewers, reserving marinade. Grill to desired degree of doneness, turning and basting with marinade frequently, about 10 minutes for medium. Mound rice on platter. Top with kebabs. Serve immediately.

Pan-fried Lamb Chops with Cognac-Butter Sauce

6 servings

½ cup dry red wine
½ cup unsalted beef broth

3 tablespoons vegetable oil
12 1-inch-thick loin lamb chops, trimmed of all fat
   Salt and freshly ground pepper

3 tablespoons minced shallot
3 garlic cloves, minced
¼ cup Cognac
1 cup (2 sticks) well-chilled unsalted butter, cut into tablespoon pieces
   Watercress

Simmer wine and broth in heavy small saucepan until reduced to ½ cup.

Heat oil in heavy large skillet over medium-high heat. Add lamb and cook about 4 minutes on each side for medium-rare, sprinkling with salt and pepper after turning. Transfer lamb to heated platter and tent with foil.

Pour off all but 1 tablespoon fat in pan. Add shallot and garlic and cook over medium-low heat until tender, stirring frequently, about 3 minutes. Spoon off any fat. Add Cognac, increase heat and bring to boil, scraping up any browned bits. Add wine mixture. Boil until reduced to 3 tablespoons liquid. Remove pan from heat and whisk in 2 tablespoons butter. Set pan over low heat and whisk in remaining butter 1 tablespoon at a time, removing pan from heat briefly if drops of melted butter appear. (If sauce breaks down at any time, remove from heat and whisk in 2 tablespoons cold butter.) Whisk any liquid on lamb platter into sauce. Season with salt and pepper. Spoon sauce over lamb. Garnish with watercress.

Savory Sautéed Lamb Chops

2 servings; can be doubled or tripled

2 large 1-inch-thick lamb shoulder chops
1 garlic clove, crushed
¼ cup olive oil
1 bay leaf, crumbled
½ teaspoon dried savory, crumbled
   Freshly ground pepper

1½ teaspoons butter
   Salt

1 garlic clove, minced
⅓ cup dry red wine
⅔ cup unsalted beef broth
¼ teaspoon Dijon mustard
1 tablespoon butter, cut into 3 pieces
¼ teaspoon dried savory, crumbled

Pat lamb dry and score edges. Rub all over with crushed garlic. Place in small dish. Combine oil, bay leaf, ½ teaspoon savory and pepper. Pour over lamb. Let stand at least 30 minutes.

Melt 1½ teaspoons butter in heavy medium skillet over medium-high heat. Remove lamb from marinade and sprinkle with salt. Add to skillet and cook to desired degree of doneness, about 4½ minutes per side for medium-rare. Transfer to heated plate. Tent with foil to keep warm.

Pour off all but film of drippings from skillet. Add minced garlic and stir over low heat 30 seconds. Add wine, increase heat and bring to boil, scraping up any browned bits. Boil until reduced to glaze, about 1½ minutes. Add broth and boil until syrupy, about 5 minutes (near end of cooking time, add any juices exuded from lamb). Whisk in mustard, then butter pieces and boil until emulsified. Mix in ¼ teaspoon savory. Season with salt and pepper. Pour over lamb and serve.

Lamb Chops Korabiak

4 servings

¼ cup (½ stick) butter or margarine
6 to 10 mushrooms, sliced
2 to 3 green onions, sliced

2 large or 4 small lamb chops
1 teaspoon minced fresh rosemary or
½ teaspoon dried, crumbled

Salt and freshly ground pepper
Garlic powder
1 cup dry red wine

Melt half of butter in large skillet over medium-high heat. Add mushroom and onion and sauté until tender, about 5 to 10 minutes. Remove and keep warm.

Melt remaining butter in same skillet over medium-high heat. Sprinkle chops with rosemary, salt, pepper and garlic powder. Add to skillet and sauté until browned on both sides, about 5 minutes. Reduce heat to medium and continue cooking until tender. Transfer lamb chops to heated platter. Pour wine into skillet and cook over medium-high heat, scraping up any browned bits clinging to bottom of pan, until liquid is reduced by ⅓. Spoon vegetables over chops and top with sauce.

Lamb with Eggplant Tahini

6 servings

4 pounds lamb neck slices or blade chops (about ¾ inch thick), trimmed
½ cup all purpose flour
½ teaspoon salt
¼ teaspoon freshly ground pepper
2 tablespoons (¼ stick) unsalted butter
2 tablespoons olive oil
½ cup dry white wine
3 cups (about) chicken stock
8 fresh dill sprigs
6 black peppercorns

2 fresh mint sprigs
2 2-inch lemon peel strips

2 medium eggplants (about 2 pounds total)
¼ cup tahini (sesame seed paste)
¼ cup plain yogurt
¼ cup whipping cream
1 tablespoon lemon juice
3 small garlic cloves, minced

Cherry tomatoes, parsley and lemon slices

Pat lamb dry. Combine flour, salt and pepper. Dredge lamb in seasoned flour, shaking off excess. Melt butter with oil in heavy large deep skillet over medium-high heat. Add lamb in batches and brown on all sides (place cooked lamb on platter). Return lamb to skillet along with any exuded juices. Add wine and enough stock to cover lamb. Tie dill, peppercorns, mint and peel in cheesecloth. Add to skillet. Bring to simmer, cover and cook until lamb is tender, adjusting heat so liquid bubbles gently, 1 to 1½ hours.

Meanwhile, preheat oven to 400°F. Pierce eggplant. Bake until very soft, about 45 minutes. Cool slightly; peel. Puree in processor. Blend in tahini, yogurt, whipping cream, lemon juice and garlic using on/off turns until smooth, scraping down sides of bowl. Transfer eggplant tahini to serving bowl.

Set lamb on platter and cover with foil. Discard cheesecloth bag. Degrease cooking liquid. Whisk ½ cup liquid into eggplant tahini. Adjust seasoning. Strain remaining cooking liquid into heavy medium saucepan. Boil until sauce is reduced to 1½ cups.

Ladle sauce over lamb. Garnish with tomatoes, parsley and lemon and serve. Pass eggplant tahini separately.

Curried Lamb Shanks

A terrific dinner party dish.

6 servings

Curried Lamb Shanks
    6 lamb shanks, each cracked into
        3 pieces
    6 tablespoons all purpose flour
 1¼ teaspoons salt
    ¼ teaspoon freshly ground pepper
    8 tablespoons clarified butter

    2 large onions, chopped
    ¼ cup minced fresh ginger
    4 large garlic cloves, minced
 1¼ teaspoons ground coriander
 1¼ teaspoons ground cumin
 1¼ teaspoons ground turmeric
    ¾ teaspoon cinnamon
    ½ teaspoon cayenne pepper
    ¼ teaspoon ground cloves
 2½ cups chicken stock
    2 16-ounce cans tomatoes, undrained

Rice and Pine Nut Pilaf
    3 tablespoons clarified butter
 1½ cups long-grain rice
    ⅓ cup coarsely chopped pine nuts
    ¼ cup currants
    ½ teaspoon slivered orange peel
    ¼ teaspoon salt
    3 cups chicken stock

    1 cup whipping cream

    ¼ cup minced fresh cilantro

For lamb shanks: Pat meat dry. Combine flour, ¼ teaspoon salt and pepper. Dredge lamb in seasoned flour, shaking off excess. Heat 6 tablespoons clarified butter in Dutch oven over medium-high heat. Add lamb in batches and brown on all sides. Transfer lamb to large bowl.

Add remaining 2 tablespoons clarified butter to Dutch oven and heat over medium-low heat. Add onions and cook until soft and lightly browned, stirring occasionally, about 10 minutes. Add ginger and garlic and stir until golden, 3 to 4 minutes. Mix in remaining 1 teaspoon salt, coriander, cumin, turmeric, cinnamon, cayenne and cloves. Blend in stock and undrained tomatoes and bring to boil, breaking up tomatoes with spoon. Return lamb to Dutch oven along with any juices in bowl. Reduce heat, cover and simmer until lamb is tender, adjusting heat so cooking liquid bubbles gently, about 2 hours.

Meanwhile, prepare pilaf: Heat clarified butter in heavy medium skillet over medium heat. Add rice and pine nuts and stir until rice is translucent and pine nuts are golden brown, about 5 minutes. Stir in currants, orange peel and salt. Blend in broth and bring to simmer. Cook *uncovered* until small holes appear on surface of rice, about 20 minutes. Reduce heat to low, cover and let steam 5 minutes.

Remove lamb from Dutch oven and cover with foil. Degrease cooking liquid. Stir in cream and boil until reduced to 3 cups. Return lamb to Dutch oven to heat through.

Mound lamb on platter. Garnish with cilantro. Pass pilaf separately.

Lamb Paillards with Tarragon and Garlic

3 to 4 servings

 1½ pounds ½-inch-thick lamb steaks
        cut from boned leg of lamb,
        trimmed
        Salt and freshly ground pepper
    2 tablespoons (¼ stick) unsalted
        butter
    1 tablespoon vegetable oil

    6 garlic cloves, minced
    ⅓ cup tarragon wine vinegar

    1 cup rich beef stock (preferably
        homemade)
    2 teaspoons tomato paste
    6 tablespoons (¾ stick) well-chilled
        unsalted butter, cut into 6 pieces
    1 tablespoon minced fresh tarragon
        or 1 teaspoon dried, crumbled

Cut large lamb steaks in half crosswise. Push into oval shapes. Pound each piece between 2 sheets of plastic wrap to thickness of ¼ inch, using flat meat pounder or rolling pin and retaining oval shape. *(Can be prepared 4 hours ahead. Cover tightly and refrigerate. Bring to room temperature before continuing.)*

Preheat oven to 275°F. Sprinkle lamb with salt and pepper. Melt 1 tablespoon butter with oil in heavy large skillet over high heat. Add half of lamb and cook until brown but still pink inside, about 1 minute per side. Arrange in single layer on ovenproof platter, cover and keep warm in oven. Repeat with remaining lamb.

Discard fat from skillet. Add 1 tablespoon butter and melt over low heat. Add garlic and stir 30 seconds. Add vinegar, increase heat to medium-high and boil until reduced to 3 tablespoons, scraping up any browned bits. Add stock and any juices accumulated on lamb platter. Boil until reduced to ½ cup, stirring frequently, about 6 minutes. Transfer sauce to heavy small saucepan. Whisk in tomato paste and bring to simmer. Remove from heat and whisk in 2 pieces of butter. Set pan over low heat and whisk in remaining butter 1 piece at a time, lifting pan from heat briefly if drops of melted butter appear. (If sauce breaks down at any time, remove from heat and whisk in 2 tablespoons cold butter.) Remove sauce from heat and stir in tarragon. Adjust seasoning. Pour sauce over lamb and serve.

Basque Burgers

6 servings

1½	pounds ground lamb
1	large yellow onion, diced
1	large red bell pepper, seeded and diced
2	tablespoons prepared mint sauce

1	tablespoon green peppercorns
1	teaspoon freshly ground pepper
½	teaspoon salt
½	teaspoon dried tarragon, crumbled
6	hamburger buns, toasted

Preheat broiler. Combine all ingredients except hamburger buns in large bowl. Shape into 6 patties. Broil 5 inches from heat source to desired doneness, 5 to 6 minutes per side for rare. Arrange on toasted buns.

Old-fashioned Irish Stew

Americans usually use lamb shoulder for Irish stew, but in Ireland neck slices are the thing. And here is some advice every good Irish cook heeds: "A stew boiled is a stew spoiled," meaning, keep the kettle at a simmer.

6 servings

3	pounds 1-inch-thick slices lamb neck, fat trimmed and reserved
4	medium onions, thinly sliced
1	medium onion, chopped
1	pound medium carrots, peeled, halved crosswise and quartered lengthwise

1	pound medium boiling potatoes, one sliced thinly, remainder quartered
3	cups lamb or beef stock
4	tablespoons minced fresh parsley
	Salt and freshly ground pepper

Mince lamb fat. Cook in heavy Dutch oven over high heat until fat renders, stirring frequently, about 5 minutes.

Strain drippings and return to Dutch oven. Heat over medium-high heat. Pat lamb dry, add in batches (do not crowd) and cook until brown, about 5 minutes per side. Transfer to large bowl using slotted spoon. Add sliced and chopped onions, carrots and sliced potato to pan and cook until light brown, stirring frequently, about 5 minutes. Return lamb to pan, spooning vegetables on top. Add stock. Reduce heat, cover and simmer gently 1 hour. Add quartered potatoes, pushing into liquid. Cover and continue to simmer until potatoes and lamb are tender when pierced with fork, about 35 minutes.

Drain liquid from pan into heavy large skillet; degrease cooking liquid. Boil until reduced by half, about 15 minutes. Return to stew. Mix in 2 tablespoons parsley. Season with salt and pepper. Ladle stew onto heated platter. Sprinkle with remaining parsley and serve.

Greek Lamb and Potato Stew

6 servings

2 tablespoons vegetable oil
2½ pounds lamb stew meat, cut into 2-inch cubes
2 medium onions, chopped
½ medium green bell pepper, finely chopped
2 garlic cloves, minced
½ teaspoon sweet paprika
¼ teaspoon ground cumin

1 16-ounce can tomatoes, crushed (juice reserved)
10 small white or red potatoes (unpeeled)
1 tablespoon minced fresh parsley
Salt and freshly ground pepper

1 pound green beans, cut into thirds

Heat oil in Dutch oven over medium-high heat. Add lamb, onions, bell pepper, garlic, paprika and cumin and cook until meat and onions are browned, stirring frequently. Add tomatoes with juice, potatoes and parsley. Season with salt and pepper. Reduce heat, cover and simmer until meat is tender, about 1¾ hours.

Add beans to stew and simmer until tender, about 15 minutes. Serve hot.

Pork

Roast Loin of Pork in Lemon-Garlic Marinade

6 servings

1 2½-pound boned and tied pork loin, ribs reserved
½ cup olive oil
½ cup fresh lemon juice

2 to 4 garlic cloves, minced
Freshly ground pepper

Salt

Place pork and ribs in shallow glass dish. Slowly whisk oil into lemon juice. Pour over meat. Sprinkle with garlic and generous amount of pepper. Cover and refrigerate 24 hours, turning occasionally.

Bring pork to room temperature. Preheat oven to 325°F. Arrange ribs meat side up in shallow roasting pan just large enough to accommodate in single layer. Sprinkle with salt. Set roast atop ribs. Sprinkle with salt. Roast until thermometer inserted in thickest part of meat registers 170°F, about 2 hours, basting frequently with marinade and pan drippings. Transfer pork to cutting board. Remove strings and tent pork with foil. Continue cooking ribs until crisp and brown, about 20 minutes. Cut pork into thin slices. Cut ribs apart; serve with roast.

Aromatic Orange Pork Kebabs

To enhance the flavor, add mesquite, pear, apple, peach, cherry, chestnut or hickory wood to the barbecue. The Indonesian-inspired marinade is also very good with duck.

8 servings

Orange Marinade
- 2 2-inch pieces cinnamon stick
- 2 tablespoons fennel seeds
- ½ teaspoon whole black peppercorns
  Peel (orange part only) and juice from 4 juice oranges
- ¾ cup frozen orange juice concentrate, thawed
- ½ cup prepared sharp Chinese mustard
- ¼ cup honey
- 2 teaspoons red wine vinegar

- 1 4-pound pork Boston butt, cut into 1-inch chunks

- 3 juice oranges, thinly sliced, then quartered
  Salt and freshly ground pepper

  Peel from 1 orange (orange part only) removed with vegetable peeler
  Freshly cooked rice

For marinade: Grind cinnamon, fennel and peppercorns to coarse powder in blender or spice mill. Cut peel from 4 oranges into julienne. Mix with spice powder, juice from 4 oranges, orange juice concentrate, mustard, honey and vinegar in large bowl.

Add pork to marinade, tossing to coat. Cover and refrigerate 8 to 12 hours.

Prepare 16 bamboo skewers by soaking in water for 1 hour before using.

Preheat oven to 325°F. Drain pork, reserving marinade. Pat pork dry, pressing spices and orange peel into meat. Alternate pork and orange slices on skewers. Sprinkle with salt and pepper. Arrange on rack set in large shallow pan. Roast pork until tender, turning occasionally, about 40 minutes.

Prepare barbecue with medium-hot coals. Add orange peel from remaining orange to coals. Brush pork with reserved marinade. Grill on all sides until brown. Arrange kebabs on bed of rice and serve.

Drunken Chops

4 servings

- 4 pork loin chops, ½-inch thick
- ½ lemon
  Salt and freshly ground pepper

- 1 teaspoon dried rosemary, crumbled
- 1 tablespoon vegetable oil
- ½ cup dry red wine

Arrange chops in dish. Squeeze lemon juice over each and season with salt and pepper. Sprinkle rosemary evenly over top. Heat oil in large skillet over medium-high heat. Add chops and brown, turning once, about 15 minutes. Pour wine over chops. Cover and simmer, turning once, until meat tests done, about 10 to 15 minutes. Transfer chops to serving platter and keep warm. Increase heat to high and boil liquid remaining in skillet until reduced to 3 or 4 tablespoons. Pour over chops. Serve immediately.

Pork Chops with Beer and Ginger

4 servings

- 4 1-inch-thick pork loin chops
- 1½ teaspoons ground ginger
  Salt and freshly ground pepper

- 3 tablespoons vegetable oil
- 2¼ cups pilsner beer

- 1 tablespoon dry breadcrumbs

Pat pork dry. Using sharp knife, slash edges several times. Sprinkle pork with ginger, salt and pepper.

Heat oil in heavy large skillet over medium-high heat. Add pork and brown on both sides. Add beer and bring to boil. Reduce heat, cover and simmer until juices run clear when pork is pierced with knife, turning occasionally, about 30 minutes.

Transfer pork to warm platter. Degrease pan juices. Add breadcrumbs to juices. Increase heat and boil until slightly thickened, scraping up browned bits. Adjust seasoning. Pour sauce over pork. Serve immediately.

Orange-glazed Pork Chops

4 servings

4 **pork loin chops (about 1½ pounds total)**
Salt and freshly ground pepper
½ **cup all purpose flour**

1 **tablespoon butter**

½ **cup fresh orange juice**
½ **cup dry white wine**
2 **tablespoons orange marmalade**
Orange slices and watercress (garnish)

Season pork chops with salt and freshly ground pepper. Dredge chops lightly in flour, shaking off excess.

Melt butter in heavy large skillet over medium heat. Add chops and cook, turning frequently, until golden brown, about 3 to 5 minutes per side. Stir in orange juice, wine and marmalade. Cover, reduce heat to low and simmer gently 20 to 25 minutes, turning once. Transfer chops to platter and keep warm. Continue cooking sauce until thickened, about 5 minutes. Spoon sauce over chops. Garnish with orange slices and watercress and serve.

Pecan-crusted Pork Cutlets with Ginger Mayonnaise

Japanese-style steamed rice is all you need to serve with this creative main course.

8 servings

2 **pounds boneless pork cutlets, trimmed**
⅓ **cup Sherry**
⅓ **cup soy sauce**
4 **medium green onions, minced**
3 **tablespoons minced peeled ginger**

2 **cups fine dry breadcrumbs**
1 **cup finely chopped pecans (3 ounces)**

All purpose flour
2 **eggs, beaten to blend**

Peanut oil
Green onion fans
Ginger Mayonnaise*

Pound pork between sheets of waxed paper to ¼-inch thickness; pat dry. Blend Sherry, soy sauce, green onions and ginger in large nonaluminum bowl. Add pork. Cover and refrigerate at least 2 hours or overnight.

Drain pork; pat dry. Mix breadcrumbs and pecans. Dredge pork in flour, shaking off excess. Dip into eggs. Dredge in breadcrumb mixture, pressing to adhere. Arrange pork on platter. Refrigerate at least 30 minutes.

Heat 1 inch of oil in heavy large skillet over medium-high heat. Cook pork in batches (do not crowd) until crisp and brown, about 3 minutes per side. Arrange on platter. Garnish with green onion fans. Serve immediately. Pass mayonnaise separately.

*Ginger Mayonnaise

Makes about 1⅓ cups

1 1-inch piece ginger, peeled
1 large garlic clove
2 egg yolks, room temperature
4 teaspoons cider vinegar
¼ teaspoon salt
¾ cup plus 2½ tablespoons peanut oil

1½ tablespoons oriental sesame oil
4 drops hot chili oil**
1 Italian plum tomato, seeded and diced
1 small green onion, minced

Mince ginger and garlic finely in processor. Add yolks, vinegar and salt and blend until smooth. Combine oils. With machine running, add oil mixture through feed tube in slow stream and mix until thickened, about 1½ minutes. Transfer to bowl. Stir in tomato and green onion. Cover and refrigerate at least 1 hour. *(Can be prepared 8 hours ahead.)*

**Available at oriental markets and many supermarkets.

Pork Scallops with Greek Eggplant and Peppers

4 servings

1 1-pound eggplant, peeled and cut into 1½x⅛x⅛-inch strips
1 tablespoon salt
1 pound boneless center loin pork, trimmed and cut across grain into about twelve ⅜-inch slices

3 tablespoons olive oil
3 large red bell peppers, seeded and cut into ⅛-inch-wide strips
1 large onion, halved and sliced ⅛ inch thick
1 large garlic clove, minced

Pinch of ground allspice
Pinch of cinnamon
4 to 5 tablespoons fresh lemon juice
Salt and freshly ground pepper

1 cup all purpose flour
2 tablespoons clarified butter

3 tablespoons butter
1 medium garlic clove, minced
1 teaspoon fresh oregano or ⅓ teaspoon dried, crumbled

Toss eggplant and 1 tablespoon salt in colander; let drain 30 minutes. Pound pork slices between sheets of waxed paper to ⅛-inch thickness.

Rinse eggplant and pat dry. Heat 2 tablespoons olive oil in heavy large skillet over medium-high heat. Add pepper strips and onion and sauté until onion begins to soften, about 4 minutes. Add eggplant and sauté until tender, about 5 minutes. Mix in 1 garlic clove, allspice and cinnamon and sauté 2 minutes. Sprinkle with 2 tablespoons lemon juice, salt and pepper. Divide mixture among 4 heated dinner plates. Place in oven on lowest setting. Wipe skillet clean.

Pat pork dry and flour lightly, shaking off excess. Heat 1 tablespoon olive oil with clarified butter in skillet over medium-high heat. Cook pork in batches (do not crowd) until just cooked through, about 10 seconds per side. Sprinkle with salt and pepper. Divide among plates and return to oven.

Pour off fat from skillet. Wipe clean with paper towels. Add 3 tablespoons butter and melt over medium-low heat. Add 1 garlic clove and sauté until soft, 3 to 4 minutes. Stir in oregano and cook until aromatic, about 1 minute. Add 2 to 3 tablespoons lemon juice. Taste and adjust seasoning. Drizzle over pork. Serve immediately.

Chimichangas

Makes 10

2 pounds pork loin, trimmed and cut into 1-inch cubes
2½ cups (about) water

4 canned green chilies, diced
2 medium garlic cloves, minced
3 tablespoons red wine vinegar
½ teaspoon cumin
½ teaspoon dried oregano, crumbled
Salt and freshly ground pepper

Butter
10 8-inch flour tortillas
Sour cream
Guacamole
Thinly sliced lettuce
Radishes

Cover pork with water in 3-quart saucepan. Cover, cook over medium heat 2 hours.

Remove cover. Increase heat to medium-high and boil until almost all liquid is absorbed, 18 to 20 minutes. Cool to room temperature. Drain pork and shred with fork. Transfer to large bowl. Add chilies, garlic, vinegar, cumin, oregano, salt and pepper. Cover and refrigerate overnight.

Preheat oven to 475°F. Reheat pork mixture in medium saucepan over low heat. Generously butter 1 side of tortillas. Place buttered side down in large skillet over medium-high heat and fry until soft, about 30 seconds. Remove from skillet. Spoon ½ cup pork mixture in center of uncooked side. Fold edges toward center and tuck ends under, as for burrito. Arrange seam side down in large baking dish. Repeat with remaining tortillas and pork. Bake until golden brown, about 20 minutes. Top each with dollop of sour cream and guacamole. Garnish with lettuce and radishes.

Sautéed Pork Tenderloin with Peaches

6 servings

3 pork tenderloins (about 2¼ pounds total), trimmed and cut against grain into 18 pieces
All purpose flour seasoned with salt and freshly ground pepper
Vegetable oil
½ cup peach or apricot brandy
1 cup beef stock

1 cup (2 sticks) well-chilled unsalted butter, cut into tablespoons
3 ripe peaches (unpeeled), cut into wedges
Pinch of cinnamon
Pinch of ground allspice
Pinch of freshly grated nutmeg

Pat pork dry. Dredge in seasoned flour, shaking off excess. Heat thin layer of oil in heavy large skillet over medium heat. Add pork and cook on both sides until no pink remains, turning frequently. Remove from skillet; keep warm. Pour off fat from skillet. Tilt skillet. Add brandy, heat and ignite. When flames subside, add stock. Boil until reduced by ⅔. Remove from heat and whisk in 2 tablespoons butter. Return to low heat and whisk in remaining butter 1 tablespoon at a time. Add peaches and heat through. Season sauce with cinnamon, allspice and nutmeg. Arrange pork on platter. Spoon sauce over. Serve immediately.

Pork with Fennel, New Potatoes and Onion

6 servings

3 pounds pork tenderloin, trimmed and cut into 1-inch cubes
1 teaspoon salt
  Freshly ground pepper
2 tablespoons vegetable oil

1 medium onion, quartered
2 large garlic cloves
¾ cup plus 2 tablespoons dry white wine
¾ cup chicken stock
1½ teaspoons dried thyme, crumbled

1 small fennel bulb (8 to 10 ounces),* feathery greens discarded and bulb cut into feed tube lengths

1 large leek, white part cut into feed tube lengths and green part reserved

2 tablespoons all purpose flour

1 pound red new potatoes, cut into 1¼-inch pieces (unpeeled)
3 tablespoons snipped fresh chives (garnish)

Position rack in center of oven and preheat to 350°F. Pat meat dry. Season with salt and pepper. Heat oil in heavy 4-quart flameproof baking dish over high heat. Brown meat on all sides in batches (do not crowd). Transfer to large plate using slotted spoon. Pour off fat. Set baking dish aside.

With processor machine running, drop onion and garlic through feed tube and mince finely. Place baking dish over medium-high heat. Stir in contents of work bowl, scraping up any browned bits in bottom of dish. Blend in meat, ¾ cup wine, stock and thyme and bring to boil. Cover, transfer to oven and bake 1½ hours.

Insert medium slicer blade in processor. Stand fennel and white part of leek upright in feed tube and slice, using medium pressure.

Mix flour and remaining 2 tablespoons wine in small bowl until smooth. Stir into meat mixture. Add fennel and leek, stirring gently into liquid. Cover, return to oven and bake 15 minutes.

Meanwhile, cook potatoes in large saucepan of boiling salted water until just tender, about 8 minutes. Drain. Cut reserved leek greens into ¼-inch slices. Gently mix potatoes and leek greens into casserole. Cover and bake 15 minutes. Adjust seasoning. Garnish with chives and serve immediately.

*If unavailable, substitute 10 ounces celery stalks, strings removed, and 2 teaspoons fennel seed. Proceed as with fennel.

Country-style Pork Ribs with Sauerkraut

Cook this hearty dish in the microwave to save time.

6 servings

3 pounds pork loin country-style ribs, trimmed of fat
7 cups water
1½ pounds fresh sauerkraut, rinsed and drained

1 16-ounce jar sweet-sour red cabbage, undrained
1 medium onion, chopped
  Salt and freshly ground pepper

Arrange ribs in 4-quart baking dish. Add water. Cover and cook in microwave on High 20 minutes. Drain ribs well and set aside. Combine sauerkraut and red cabbage in shallow 2½-quart baking dish. Arrange ribs over top, with thickest portion facing outside of dish and any smaller ribs in center. Sprinkle with onion and season with salt and pepper. Cover with waxed paper and cook on Medium (50 percent power) 15 minutes. Check for even cooking, shifting slower-cooking ribs to outside of dish if necessary. Turn ribs over and repeat seasoning. Cover dish with foil. Let stand at room temperature until ribs test done, about 10 minutes.

Baked Spareribs and Sauerkraut

4 to 6 servings

1 tablespoon butter
1 medium onion, sliced
2 27-ounce cans sauerkraut, undrained
2⅓ cups water
1 medium baking potato, peeled and grated
6 tablespoons firmly packed dark brown sugar

4 pounds pork spareribs
½ teaspoon salt
½ teaspoon sweet paprika
¼ teaspoon freshly ground pepper

½ cup water

Melt butter in 4-quart saucepan over medium-high heat. Add onion and cook until transparent, stirring occasionally, about 5 minutes. Add sauerkraut with juices and 2⅓ cups water. Stir in potato. Mix in brown sugar. Reduce heat to low and cook 15 minutes, stirring occasionally.

Meanwhile, season ribs with salt, paprika and pepper. Separate ribs using sharp knife. Brown in heavy large dry skillet over medium-high heat, 10 to 12 minutes.

Preheat oven to 350°F. Spread ¼ of sauerkraut mixture in bottom of large baking dish. Top with ¼ of ribs. Repeat layering, ending with ribs. Add ½ cup water to skillet and deglaze over low heat, scraping up brown bits. Pour over ribs. Cover and bake until ribs are tender, about 2 hours. Degrease if necessary. Serve immediately.

Fresh Ham with Garlic Chili Sauce

4 servings

4 small fresh red chilies
4 jalapeño chilies

10 cups water
¾ pound pork shoulder butt, room temperature, cut into 2x3-inch chunks

5 large garlic cloves
5 teaspoons water

2 teaspoons soy sauce
2 teaspoons dark soy sauce
1 teaspoon distilled white vinegar
1 teaspoon oriental sesame oil
1 teaspoon sugar
½ teaspoon salt

1 teaspoon hot chili oil*

Using scissors, cut tips open on 3 red and 3 green chilies. Cut up side of each chili to ¼ inch from stem. Repeat 6 times on each chili. Combine chilies, water to cover and 10 ice cubes in bowl. Chill until chilies open, 2 hours.

Bring 10 cups water to boil in large saucepan. Add pork. Cover and cook until pork is tender and no pink remains, about 25 minutes. Drain; rinse pork under cold water 1 minute. Drain. Cover; cool to room temperature.

Mash garlic with 3 teaspoons water to paste in mortar with pestle. Transfer to bowl. Add remaining 2 teaspoons water, soy sauces, vinegar, sesame oil, sugar and salt. Cut remaining 2 chilies crosswise into 3 pieces. Add to sauce.

Drain opened chilies. Slice pork as thinly as possible. Arrange on platter. Garnish with chilies. Drizzle chili oil into sauce. Spoon sauce over pork.

*Available at oriental markets.

Glazed Ham Steak

2 servings; can be doubled or tripled

1   8- to 10-ounce smoked ham steak

6   tablespoons pure maple syrup
2½   teaspoons Dijon mustard (preferably coarse-grained)
2   teaspoons butter

1   teaspoon minced fresh thyme or ¼ teaspoon dried, crumbled

Preheat broiler. Broil ham steak until first side is hot, about 3 minutes.

Meanwhile, boil syrup, mustard and butter in heavy small saucepan until reduced to ¼ cup, about 3 minutes.

Turn ham over. Spread with maple mixture. Sprinkle with thyme. Broil until hot, about 1 minute. Cut steak in half and serve immediately.

Italian Sausage and Peppers

Prepare this easy main dish in the microwave.

6 to 8 servings

1   large green bell pepper, cored, seeded and cut into wedges
1   medium onion, cut into wedges and separated
1   tablespoon oil
1   pound sweet Italian sausages

1   14½-ounce can Italian whole tomatoes, drained and sliced
½   pound mushrooms, sliced
3   tablespoons red wine
½   teaspoon dried oregano, crumbled
    Minced fresh parsley (garnish)

Mix green pepper, onion and oil in 2-quart round baking dish. Cook in microwave on High 5 minutes. Remove vegetables from dish and set aside. Add sausages to dish with just enough water to cover. Cover and cook on High 10 minutes. Pour off liquid; drain sausages on paper towel. Cut sausages in half crosswise. Return to dish and cook on High, uncovered, 3 to 5 minutes, shifting sausages at outside of dish to center as they begin to brown. Pour off fat.

Return green pepper and onion to dish with tomatoes, mushrooms, wine and oregano. Cover and cook on Medium (50 percent power) until mushrooms are tender, about 10 to 11 minutes. Garnish with parsley. Serve hot.

Polenta and Sausage Casserole

4 to 6 servings

1 8½-ounce package corn muffin mix
½ cup grated Parmesan cheese

1 tablespoon vegetable oil
1 pound sweet Italian sausage links

1 large onion, chopped
1 garlic clove, chopped
1 1-pound can whole tomatoes, drained and chopped (reserve ½ cup liquid)

3 ounces tomato paste
½ teaspoon dried oregano, crumbled
Salt and freshly ground pepper

6 to 8 ounces mozzarella or Fontina cheese, cut into ⅛-inch slices

Grease 2-quart baking dish. Prepare corn muffin mix according to package directions, adding Parmesan cheese to batter. Turn into prepared dish, spreading evenly.

Preheat oven to 375°F. Heat oil in large skillet over medium heat. Add sausage and cook, turning frequently, until browned on all sides, about 13 to 15 minutes. Slice sausage in half lengthwise and set aside.

Add onion and garlic to skillet. Increase heat to medium-high and sauté until tender, about 7 to 10 minutes. Add tomatoes and liquid, tomato paste, oregano, salt and pepper and continue cooking until sauce is thickened, about 4 minutes.

Arrange half of sausage over corn muffin batter. Spread tomato sauce over evenly. Top with remaining sausage. Bake 15 minutes. Top with cheese and continue baking until cheese melts, about 10 minutes. Serve hot.

Sausage Choucroute

This is even better if made one day ahead. Serve with crusty French bread.

2 servings; can be doubled or tripled

1 pound assorted sausages, such as kielbasa, knockwurst and bratwurst
6 ounces slab or sliced bacon, cut into ¾-inch squares

1 large onion, sliced
1 large carrot, peeled and sliced
1 pound sauerkraut, drained and rinsed

1 cup chicken stock
½ cup dry white wine
10 juniper berries or ¼ cup gin
2 bay leaves
Salt and freshly ground pepper
Coarse-grained Dijon mustard

Halve kielbasa and knockwurst lengthwise. Cook sausages and bacon in heavy large saucepan over medium-high heat until browned and fat is rendered, turning occasionally, 10 minutes.

Transfer sausages and bacon to plate. Pour off pan drippings, reserving 3 table-spoons. Rinse saucepan if necessary. Return reserved drippings to pan. Heat over low heat. Mix in onion and carrot. Cover and cook until onion is translucent, stirring occasionally, about 10 minutes. Mix in sauerkraut. Cover and cook 10 minutes. Add stock, wine, juniper berries and bay leaves. Return sausages and bacon to pan. Bring to boil. Reduce heat, cover and simmer 45 minutes. Season with salt and pepper. Increase heat and boil uncovered until almost all liquid evaporates, about 10 minutes. Discard bay leaves. Serve with mustard.

4 ❦ Poultry

Versatile and inexpensive, chicken is the hands-down favorite of cooks around the world. It can be prepared so many different ways—in a hearty, country-style stew; as delicate fillets in an elegant sauce; or quickly stir-fried with fresh vegetables, mushrooms and other healthful ingredients.

Our easy entrée recipes represent many national and ethnic cuisines. There's Szechwan Fried Chicken (page 86) and an Oriental Chicken Stir-fry (page 76); Greek Baked Chicken Kapama (page 89); African-style Peanut Butter Chicken (page 86); Baked Chicken German Style (page 89); and a French Chicken Stew with Fennel and Pernod (page 87).

Dieters will appreciate innovative but low-calorie dishes such as Chicken Chili with Yogurt and Avocado Topping (page 77), Chicken Scallops with Mustard Glaze (page 83) and Curried Chicken with Green Cabbage and Red Apple (page 84). For casual, home-style suppers, nothing could be easier or more satisfying than Vineyard Chicken (page 80) or Honey-Pecan Fried Chicken (page 85). And for effortlessly elegant dinners, Roast Chicken with Garlic Croutons (page 90) and Chicken Breasts with Chinese Mushrooms (page 80) are two dishes that take a minimum of preparation time.

Not to be overlooked in this chapter are recipes using turkey. A purchased roasted turkey leg or leftover turkey can be easily transformed into a flavorful Turkey Hash with Sweet Potatoes and Turnips (page 92). And thinly sliced turkey breast cooks quickly to make the sophisticated Crisp Turkey Paillards with Capers (page 92).

Stir-fry of Chicken, Broccoli and Red Bell Pepper

Have all ingredients prepared and all implements at the ready before starting this quick and easy dish.

4 servings

1 pound skinned and boned chicken breasts, trimmed
6 cups broccoli florets (from about 2 pounds broccoli)

Nonstick vegetable oil spray
1 tablespoon olive oil
2 large red or green bell peppers, quartered lengthwise, cored, seeded and cut crosswise into ⅜-inch-wide strips
1 large onion, halved lengthwise and cut crosswise into ¼-inch-thick slices

2 large garlic cloves, minced
1 teaspoon dried basil, crumbled
½ teaspoon dried thyme, crumbled
½ teaspoon freshly ground pepper
¼ teaspoon dried rosemary, crumbled
½ teaspoon salt
4 tablespoons freshly grated Parmesan cheese

Pound chicken breasts between sheets of waxed paper to thickness of ¼ inch, using mallet or flat side of cleaver. Wrap each chicken breast separately in plastic and freeze until firm but not solid. Cut chicken crosswise into ⅜-inch-wide strips. Cover broccoli with cold water in medium bowl.

Coat heavy large skillet with vegetable spray. Add olive oil and heat over high heat 1 minute. Add red peppers, onion, garlic, basil, thyme, pepper and rosemary to skillet. Stir-fry 2 minutes. Drain broccoli (do not shake off excess water) and add to skillet. Stir-fry 3 minutes. Reduce heat to medium-low, cover and steam 2 minutes. Stir in chicken and salt. Cover and steam until chicken is almost cooked through, about 1 minute. Uncover, increase heat and stir-fry until liquid reduces slightly, about 1 minute. Divide among heated plates. Top each portion with 1 tablespoon Parmesan.

Oriental Chicken Stir-fry

4 servings

2 teaspoons soy sauce
2 teaspoons dry Sherry
2 teaspoons cornstarch
2 teaspoons water
Freshly ground pepper
1½ pounds boned and skinned chicken, cut into bite-size pieces

½ cup water
2 tablespoons soy sauce
1 tablespoon dry Sherry

1 tablespoon cornstarch
1 teaspoon oriental sesame oil
¼ teaspoon sugar

1½ teaspoons vegetable oil
½ pound mushrooms, sliced
4 ounces water chestnuts, sliced
4 ounces snow peas
2½ ounces roasted unsalted cashews
Freshly cooked rice

Combine first 5 ingredients in medium bowl, stirring until cornstarch dissolves. Add chicken pieces and stir to coat. Cover and marinate 15 minutes.

Blend ½ cup water, 2 tablespoons soy sauce, 1 tablespoon Sherry, 1 tablespoon cornstarch, sesame oil and sugar in another bowl. Set aside.

Heat vegetable oil in wok or heavy large skillet over high heat. Add chicken mixture and stir-fry until chicken is opaque, about 3 minutes. Remove chicken using slotted spoon and set aside. Add mushrooms, water chestnuts and snow peas to wok and stir-fry until crisp-tender, about 3 minutes. Return chicken to wok. Stir soy sauce mixture and add. Stir until sauce boils and thickens, 1 to 2 minutes. Mix in cashews. Serve immediately over rice.

Chicken Chili with Yogurt and Avocado Topping

There is also beef in this recipe, but only a very small amount, which makes this a great low-calorie entrée.

8 servings

1 pound skinned and boned chicken breast, trimmed, cut into 1-inch cubes

2 tablespoons corn oil
4 medium onions, coarsely chopped
2 large green bell peppers, coarsely chopped
3 large garlic cloves, minced
1 teaspoon ground cumin
1 teaspoon dried oregano, crumbled
½ teaspoon ground coriander
½ teaspoon dried thyme, crumbled
½ pound lean ground round

2 bay leaves
3 tablespoons chili powder
3 1-pound cans tomatoes, undrained
2 tablespoons tomato paste
Salt and freshly ground pepper
Water (optional)

1 small avocado, peeled, pitted and cut into ¼-inch dice
Fresh lemon juice
1 cup plain lowfat yogurt
⅓ cup minced fresh cilantro or Italian parsley

Wrap chicken and freeze until firm but not solid. Grind coarsely in processor, using on/off turns.

Heat oil in heavy large Dutch oven over medium-high heat. Add onions, green peppers and garlic and cook until golden brown, stirring frequently, about 15 minutes. Mix in cumin, oregano, coriander and thyme and stir 2 minutes. Add chicken, ground round and bay leaves. Cook until meat and chicken are no longer pink, breaking up with spoon, about 5 minutes. Add chili powder. Reduce heat to medium and cook 5 minutes, stirring frequently. Add tomatoes, breaking up large pieces with spoon. Mix in tomato paste, salt and pepper. Reduce heat, cover and simmer 45 minutes, stirring occasionally. Uncover, reduce heat to lowest setting and cook 1½ hours, stirring frequently near end and adding water if necessary to prevent burning. Adjust seasoning. *(Can be prepared 1 day ahead and refrigerated.)*

Sprinkle avocado with lemon juice. Ladle chili into large soup bowls. Spoon 2 tablespoons yogurt in center of each. Top with diced avocado and minced cilantro.

Chicken Budapest with Easy Homemade Noodles

6 servings

1 tablespoon vegetable oil
3 whole chicken breasts, skinned, boned and cut into chunks
1 cup chicken stock
⅓ cup minced onion
2 tablespoons Hungarian sweet paprika
2 tablespoons minced fresh parsley

1 teaspoon garlic salt
½ teaspoon Italian herb seasoning

1 cup all purpose flour
2 eggs, beaten to blend

3 tablespoons all purpose flour
1 cup sour cream
1 tablespoon Hungarian hot paprika

Heat oil in large skillet over medium-high heat. Add chicken and stir until no longer pink, about 4 minutes. Stir in stock, onion, sweet paprika, parsley, garlic salt and Italian seasoning. Reduce heat, cover and simmer chicken 20 minutes.

Meanwhile, bring large saucepan of water to boil. Beat 1 cup flour and eggs to form thick dough. Pinch off small pieces of dough and drop into boiling water 3 or 4 at a time. Boil until noodles rise to top. Remove with slotted spoon; drain well.

Using slotted spoon, transfer cooked chicken to plate. Whisk 3 tablespoons flour into skillet and cook over medium heat until thickened, about 3 minutes. Reduce heat to low. Blend in sour cream and hot paprika. Add chicken and noodles. Stir until heated through.

Cinnamon Chicken

2 to 4 servings

4 boneless chicken breast halves
¼ teaspoon cinnamon
¼ teaspoon ground cloves
   Salt and freshly ground pepper
2 tablespoons vegetable oil
¾ cup chopped onions

2 garlic cloves, minced
¾ cup fresh orange juice
2 tablespoons raisins
1 tablespoon capers, drained and rinsed

Pat chicken dry. Season with cinnamon, cloves, salt and pepper. Heat oil in heavy large skillet over medium-high heat. Add chicken skin side down and cook until browned, 3 to 4 minutes. Add onions and garlic. Turn chicken and cook until second side is brown, stirring onions and garlic frequently, 3 to 4 minutes. Pour off oil in skillet. Add orange juice, raisins and capers to skillet. Reduce heat to low. Cover and cook until juices run clear when chicken is pierced with sharp knife, about 10 minutes.

Chicken Rosato

2 servings

2 tablespoons olive oil
¼ cup all purpose flour
1 tablespoon paprika
1 teaspoon garlic salt
4 boneless chicken breast halves

1 cup rosé
1 tablespoon fresh basil, finely minced

1 tablespoon fresh rosemary, finely minced
1 cup sour cream

1 cup freshly cooked rice
   Chopped fresh parsley

Heat oil in large skillet over medium-high heat. Combine next 3 ingredients in shallow dish. Dredge chicken in flour, shaking off excess. Add to skillet and cook until golden brown, 3 to 4 minutes per side. Remove from skillet.

Increase heat to high. Add wine, basil and rosemary and cook, stirring frequently, until liquid is reduced to ½ cup, about 10 minutes. Reduce heat to medium-high. Return chicken to skillet and cook until tender, 2 to 3 minutes. Remove using slotted spoon; keep warm. Add sour cream to skillet and stir until sauce is heated through, about 1 to 2 minutes.

Mound rice in center of serving platter and sprinkle with parsley. Pour sauce around rice. Arrange chicken atop sauce. Serve immediately.

Chicken Breasts with Balsamic Vinegar and Tomato-Pimiento Puree

4 servings

2 large whole chicken breasts,
   skinned, boned and halved
   Salt and freshly ground pepper
2 teaspoons safflower oil
3 tablespoons balsamic vinegar
1 tablespoon unsalted butter

Tomato-Pimiento Puree*
4 teaspoons snipped fresh chives

Pat chicken dry. Pound each chicken breast between 2 sheets of plastic wrap to even thickness. Season with salt and pepper. Heat oil in heavy 10-inch skillet over medium-high heat. Add chicken, cover and cook until just opaque, about 2 minutes per side. Transfer to heated platter. Tent chicken with foil; keep warm. Add vinegar to skillet and bring to boil, scraping up any browned bits. Mix in butter. Adjust seasoning.

Spoon 3 tablespoons hot tomato puree in center of each plate. Top with chicken. Drizzle vinegar sauce over chicken. Sprinkle with chives.

*Tomato-Pimiento Puree

Makes ¾ cup

1 small onion, quartered
2 large garlic cloves
3 medium tomatoes, peeled,
   quartered and seeded
2 tablespoons tomato paste

¼ teaspoon sugar
   Salt and freshly ground pepper
1 2-ounce jar pimientos (undrained)
1 teaspoon unsalted butter

With processor machine running, drop onion and garlic through feed tube and mince finely. Add tomatoes and chop using 6 to 8 on/off turns. Transfer tomato mixture to heavy 1-quart nonaluminum saucepan. Add tomato paste, sugar, salt and pepper. Simmer until very thick, stirring occasionally, about 55 minutes.

Puree tomato mixture and pimientos with liquid in processor until smooth. Return to saucepan. Mix in butter. Cook until heated through. Adjust seasoning. (*Can be prepared 5 days ahead and refrigerated or 3 months ahead and frozen.*)

Skewered Honey Lemon Chicken and Vegetables

6 servings

2 large garlic cloves
½ cup safflower oil
⅓ cup honey
⅓ cup soy sauce
⅓ cup Scotch
¾ teaspoon salt
   Freshly ground pepper

2 large lemons, scored and sliced
8 boneless chicken breast halves
   (2 pounds), cut horizontally into
   thirds, white tendons removed

24 large mushrooms, stems trimmed
12 large green onions, white part cut
   into 2-inch pieces
2 large green bell peppers, cut into
   2-inch squares
1 large red bell pepper, cut into
   2-inch squares

Parsley sprigs (garnish)

Mince garlic finely in processor. Add oil, honey, soy sauce, Scotch, salt and pepper and mix 3 seconds. Pour marinade into large plastic bag and add lemon slices. Add chicken and vegetables to marinade and refrigerate at least 6 hours or overnight, turning bag over occasionally.

Preheat indoor grill or broiler. Drain lemon, chicken and vegetables, reserving marinade. Thread each of six 10-inch skewers with piece of chicken (fold large pieces over double), lemon slice, green or red pepper square, mushroom and green onion, then repeat 3 times. Place kebabs on hot grill (or on foil-lined jelly roll pan under broiler) and cook 3 minutes on each side (for total of 12 minutes), brushing frequently with reserved marinade. Edges of chicken should be dark brown; *do not overcook.* Arrange skewers on serving platter and garnish with parsley sprigs. Serve immediately.

Vineyard Chicken

Serve this entrée with sautéed mushrooms and crisp pan-roasted potatoes.

4 servings

2 tablespoons all purpose flour
¼ teaspoon dried basil, crumbled
¼ teaspoon dried tarragon, crumbled
¼ teaspoon paprika
  Salt and freshly ground white pepper
4 chicken breast halves, boned and skinned
1 tablespoon safflower oil

1 tablespoon butter
2 small garlic cloves, minced
½ cup dry white wine
1 cup red grapes, halved and seeded
½ cup chicken stock
1 teaspoon fresh lemon juice
1 tablespoon finely chopped fresh parsley (garnish)

Mix flour, basil, tarragon, paprika, salt and pepper in large bowl. Add chicken and toss gently to coat. Heat oil with butter in heavy large skillet over medium-high heat. Stir in garlic. Add chicken and sauté on both sides until golden brown. Pour in wine. Cover and cook just until chicken is done, about 3 minutes. Add grapes, stock and lemon juice and continue cooking until heated through. Transfer chicken and grapes to heated serving platter using slotted spoon. Continue cooking sauce until reduced by half. Pour sauce over chicken. Top with parsley and serve.

Chicken Breasts with Chinese Mushrooms

Serve with rice and broccoli on a side plate. Do not add salt to the ginger-scented sauce, as these mushrooms have a high sodium content.

4 servings

2 large whole chicken breasts, halved, boned and skinned
  Melted butter
  Coarse salt
  Freshly ground white pepper

Sauce
8 medium dried Chinese mushrooms
¾ cup warm water
1½ cups chicken stock
½ cup dry white wine

1 tablespoon minced shallot
1 teaspoon minced fresh ginger
½ teaspoon minced garlic
¾ cup whipping cream
2½ tablespoons glace de viande
⅓ cup drained canned Chinese straw mushrooms
¼ cup chopped fresh chives

Prepare chicken breasts according to instructions (see page 49). Lightly brush 4 ovenproof plates with melted butter and sprinkle lightly with salt and pepper. Place chicken breasts in center of each plate. Brush lightly with butter and sprinkle with pepper. Press small piece of waxed paper on top of each breast. Set aside.

For sauce: Soak mushrooms in warm water 15 minutes. Drain well (reserving soaking liquid); squeeze out excess moisture. Remove stems and slice into strips; set caps and stems aside.

Pour soaking liquid into medium saucepan. Add chicken stock, wine, shallot, ginger and garlic and cook over medium heat until reduced to about 1 cup. *(Can be prepared several hours ahead to this point.)*

Stir in cream and glace de viande and continue cooking until sauce is slightly reduced, about 5 to 8 minutes. Add rehydrated and straw mushrooms and continue cooking until about 1 cup of sauce remains. Preheat oven to 450°F.

Blend chives into sauce. Season to taste with white pepper. Keep warm.

Bake chicken 5 minutes. Remove plates from oven and discard waxed paper. Divide sauce evenly and spoon over chicken. Serve immediately.

Chicken with Irish Whiskey Sauce

4 servings

2 tablespoons (¼ stick) unsalted butter
1 tablespoon all purpose flour
1 cup half and half
¼ cup chicken broth
1 tablespoon Irish whiskey
1 bay leaf
1 teaspoon freshly ground pepper
½ teaspoon dried basil, crumbled
½ teaspoon dried chervil, crumbled

½ teaspoon dried thyme, crumbled
¼ teaspooon dried rosemary, crumbled

16 asparagus spears, freshly cooked
4 boneless chicken breast halves, skinned and pounded to thickness of ¼ inch
8 tablespoons grated Swiss cheese

Preheat oven to 350°F. Melt butter in heavy medium saucepan over medium heat. Add flour and stir 2 minutes. Gradually whisk in half and half, broth and whiskey. Reduce heat to low. Add bay leaf, pepper, basil, chervil, thyme and rosemary and stir until thickened, 8 minutes.

Meanwhile, arrange 4 asparagus spears lengthwise over each chicken breast. Top each with 2 tablespoons sauce and 1 tablespoon cheese. Roll chicken up lengthwise and arrange seam side down in ovenproof glass baking dish. Bake until opaque, about 20 to 25 minutes.

Rewarm remaining sauce. Discard bay leaf. Transfer chicken to serving platter. Pour sauce over. Sprinkle with remaining cheese. Serve immediately.

Poached Chicken Breasts in Chèvre Cream Sauce

4 servings

2 large whole chicken breasts, skinned, boned, halved and trimmed
1 small onion, quartered
½ celery stalk, coarsely chopped
1 fresh parsley sprig
¼ bay leaf
¼ teaspoon dried thyme, crumbled

3 whole peppercorns
2 cups chicken stock (about)

¾ cup whipping cream
3½ ounces goat cheese such as Montrachet, crumbled
Thyme sprigs

Tuck ends under chicken to form compact pieces. Arrange smooth side up in saucepan just large enough to accommodate in single layer. Add onion, celery, parsley, bay leaf, thyme and peppercorns. Pour in enough stock to just cover. Bring to simmer, skimming surface. Adjust heat so liquid barely shimmers, cover and cook until chicken is just firm to touch, about 15 minutes. Transfer chicken to heated platter, using slotted spoon. Tent with foil to keep warm.

Strain cooking liquid through double thickness of moistened cheesecloth into heavy large skillet. Boil until reduced to ½ cup. Add cream and boil until reduced to ¾ cup. Reduce heat to medium. Add cheese and mix until melted. Remove foil and discard any liquid on chicken platter. Nap chicken with sauce. Garnish with thyme sprigs. Pass remaining sauce separately.

Chicken Rinaldi with Mornay Sauce

Prepare both the chicken and the easy cheese sauce in the microwave.

4 to 6 servings

3 whole chicken breasts, split, skinned and boned
  Salt and freshly ground pepper
½ cup finely chopped onion
4 tablespoons (½ stick) butter
½ cup breadcrumbs
¼ cup grated Swiss cheese
½ teaspoon paprika
⅓ cup chicken stock

Mornay Sauce
2 tablespoons (¼ stick) butter
2 tablespoons all purpose flour

½ teaspoon salt
1 cup milk
½ cup grated Swiss cheese
2 tablespoons grated Parmesan cheese
2 tablespoons dry white wine

  Finely chopped parsley (garnish)

Season chicken with salt and pepper. Combine onion and 2 tablespoons butter in 2-cup measure. Cover and cook on High until onion is tender, stirring once or twice, about 1 to 2 minutes. Melt 2 more tablespoons butter in 2-quart rectangular baking dish on High 45 seconds. Combine breadcrumbs, Swiss cheese and paprika in small bowl. Dip chicken in butter, then roll in breadcrumb mixture, covering completely. Pour chicken stock into baking dish. Arrange chicken in dish with thickest portion of pieces toward outer edge. Spoon onion mixture over chicken. Cover and cook on High for 8 more minutes. Set aside.

For sauce: Melt 2 tablespoons butter in 1-quart measure on High, 30 to 50 seconds. Blend in flour and salt. Gradually stir in milk, mixing well. Cook on High, stirring frequently, until mixture boils and thickens, about 3 to 5½ minutes. Add cheeses and wine and stir until cheese is melted. (If necessary, cook on High 30 seconds to 1 minute to melt cheese.)

Pour sauce over chicken. Cook on High until heated through, about 2½ to 3 minutes. Garnish with parsley and serve hot.

Chicken with Mustard Cream Sauce

4 to 6 servings

⅓ cup all purpose flour
  Salt and freshly ground pepper
6 boneless chicken breast halves, pounded flat
4 tablespoons (½ stick) unsalted butter

3 tablespoons chopped shallots
½ cup dry white wine
2 cups whipping cream
½ cup Dijon mustard
  Fresh parsley sprigs
  Freshly cooked rice

Mix flour, salt and pepper on plate. Pat chicken dry. Dredge in flour mixture. Melt 2 tablespoons butter in heavy large skillet over medium-high heat. Add chicken skin side down and cook until just springy to touch, about 3 minutes per side. Transfer chicken to platter. Keep warm.

Melt remaining butter in same skillet over medium heat. Add shallots and cook until translucent, stirring occasionally, about 1 minute. Increase heat to high. Add wine and bring to boil, scraping up any browned bits. Reduce heat to medium. Simmer until wine is reduced by half, about 4 minutes. Stir in cream. Continue simmering until sauce is reduced to 1½ cups. Stir in mustard. Pour sauce over chicken. Garnish with parsley. Serve immediately with rice.

Chicken Scallops with Mustard Glaze

4 servings

- 4 4-ounce skinned and boned chicken breasts, trimmed
- 3 tablespoons all purpose flour
- ½ teaspoon dried marjoram, crumbled
- ½ teaspoon dried thyme, crumbled
- ½ teaspoon freshly ground pepper

  Nonstick vegetable oil spray
- 2 tablespoons (¼ stick) unsalted butter

- ½ cup dry vermouth
- 1 cup chicken stock
- 2 tablespoons Dijon mustard
- ¼ teaspoon finely grated lemon peel
- 3 tablespoons whipping cream
  Thin lemon slices
  Watercress or Italian parsley sprigs

Pound chicken between sheets of waxed paper to thickness of ¼ inch, using mallet or flat side of cleaver. Combine flour, marjoram, thyme and pepper. Transfer 1 tablespoon seasoned flour to small bowl and reserve. Rub remainder into chicken.

Coat heavy large skillet generously with vegetable spray. Add butter and melt over medium heat. Add chicken and cook until brown, about 2 minutes per side. Transfer to plate. Add vermouth to skillet and boil until reduced to glaze, scraping up any browned bits, about 5 minutes. Mix in stock, mustard and lemon peel. Boil 2 minutes. Mix cream into reserved seasoned flour. Whisk in ¼ cup hot broth; return mixture to skillet. Simmer until thickened and smooth, stirring constantly, about 3 minutes. Return chicken to skillet, adjust heat so sauce is just shaking and cook until opaque, about 2 minutes per side. Transfer to plates. Garnish with lemon slices and watercress.

Chicken Breast Paillards with Spiced Tomato Sauce

4 servings

Tomato Sauce
- 2 tablespoons vegetable oil
- ½ medium onion, minced
- 2 garlic cloves, minced
- 1 teaspoon ground cumin
- ¼ teaspoon turmeric
- 2 pounds tomatoes, peeled, seeded and finely chopped
  Pinch of cayenne pepper
  Salt and freshly ground pepper
- 2 teaspoons tomato paste (optional)

- 4 6- to 7-ounce whole boneless chicken breasts, skinned and well trimmed
- 2½ teaspoons minced fresh cilantro

  Salt and freshly ground pepper
- 2½ tablespoons vegetable oil
- 4 small cilantro sprigs

For sauce: Heat oil in heavy large saucepan over low heat. Add onion and cook until soft, stirring occasionally, about 10 minutes. Add garlic and stir 30 seconds. Add cumin and turmeric and stir 30 seconds. Mix in tomatoes, cayenne, salt and pepper. Bring to boil. Reduce heat to low and cook until tomatoes are very soft, stirring occasionally, about 30 minutes; sauce will be chunky. Add tomato paste if brighter color is desired. *(Can be prepared 1 day ahead. Cover and refrigerate.)*

Pound each chicken breast between 2 sheets of plastic wrap to a thickness of ¼ inch, using flat meat pounder or rolling pin. *(Can be prepared 4 hours ahead. Wrap tightly and refrigerate. Bring to room temperature before continuing.)*

Preheat oven to 275°F. Just before serving, reheat sauce. Add minced cilantro. Taste and adjust seasoning. Cover sauce and keep warm.

Heat ridged grill pan or heavy large skillet over high heat until tip of chicken sizzles when touched to grill. Pat chicken dry, sprinkle with salt and pepper and brush with oil. Cook 1 or 2 chicken pieces (do not crowd) 1 minute on first side. Brush with oil and turn. Cook until just firm to touch, about 1 minute. Transfer to ovenproof platter, cover and keep warm in oven while grilling remaining chicken. Divide sauce among plates and top with chicken. Garnish with cilantro sprigs.

Curried Chicken with Green Cabbage and Red Apple

4 servings

¾ pound skinned and boned chicken breasts
  Nonstick vegetable oil spray
2 tablespoons oriental sesame oil
1 tablespoon mustard seeds
½ small cabbage, halved, cored and cut into ¼-inch-thick slices
1 large onion, halved and cut into ¼-inch-thick slices
1 medium green bell pepper, cut into matchstick julienne
1 large carrot, coarsely shredded

1 large garlic clove, minced
4 teaspoons minced fresh ginger
4 teaspoons curry powder
¼ teaspoon freshly ground pepper
¼ cup chicken stock
1 medium tart red apple (such as Winesap, Jonathan or McIntosh), quartered, cored and thinly sliced
3 tablespoons coarsely chopped fresh Italian parsley
½ teaspoon salt

Pound chicken between sheets of waxed paper to thickness of ½ inch, using mallet or flat side of cleaver. Cut crosswise into 3x½-inch strips. Coat heavy large skillet generously with vegetable spray. Add sesame oil and heat over high heat. Add chicken and stir-fry until white on outside, about 30 seconds. Remove using slotted spoon. Add mustard seeds and cook until crackling. Add cabbage, onion, green pepper, carrot, garlic, ginger, curry powder and pepper. Stir-fry 2 minutes. Return chicken to skillet. Add stock, reduce heat to medium-low, cover and cook until chicken is almost cooked through, about 2 minutes. Add apple, parsley and salt. Stir-fry until apple is heated through, about 1 minute. Serve immediately.

Chicken Paillards with Tricolored Bell Peppers

4 servings

4 6- to 7-ounce boneless chicken breast halves, skinned and trimmed

1 medium red bell pepper
1 medium green bell pepper
1 medium yellow bell pepper*
3 tablespoons olive oil
1 jalapeño chili, seeds and ribs discarded, minced
  Salt

  Freshly ground pepper
¼ cup olive oil
¼ cup all purpose flour
1 tablespoon minced fresh parsley
4 small basil sprigs

Pound each chicken breast between 2 sheets of plastic wrap to thickness of ¼ inch, using flat meat pounder or rolling pin. *(Can be prepared 4 hours ahead. Cover tightly and refrigerate. Bring to room temperature before continuing.)*

Halve bell peppers and discard seeds and ribs. Cut bell peppers into 1½x¼-inch strips. Heat 3 tablespoons oil in heavy large skillet over low heat. Add jalapeño and cook until soft, stirring occasionally, about 4 minutes. Add bell peppers and pinch of salt. Cook until tender, stirring frequently, about 15 minutes. Adjust seasoning. *(Can be prepared 1 hour ahead. Let stand at room temperature.)*

Preheat oven to 275°F. Sprinkle chicken with salt and pepper. Heat ¼ cup oil in another heavy large skillet over medium-high heat. Dust chicken with flour, shaking to remove excess. Add to skillet and cook until brown and just tender when pierced with sharp knife, about 2 minutes per side. Arrange in single layer on ovenproof platter and keep warm in oven. Repeat flouring and cooking remaining chicken. Reheat bell peppers over low heat, stirring constantly. Discard any juices accumulated on chicken platter. Spoon bell peppers around chicken, using slotted spoon. Sprinkle with parsley. Arrange basil sprig atop each chicken breast. Serve immediately.

*If yellow bell peppers are unavailable, use an additional red bell pepper.

Barbecued Chicken Wings and Spareribs

24 servings

36 chicken wings
2 slabs spareribs (about 8½ pounds total), cut crosswise into 2-inch pieces and separated
4 cups olive oil
1½ cups raspberry vinegar
½ cup fresh lemon juice

½ cup raspberry, clover or orange honey
½ cup sesame seeds
4 teaspoons cumin
2 teaspoons salt
8 garlic cloves, crushed

Arrange chicken wings and ribs in roasting pan. Mix oil, vinegar, lemon juice, honey, seeds, cumin, salt and garlic in processor to blend. Pour over chicken and ribs. Cover and refrigerate overnight, turning occasionally.

Prepare barbecue (low heat). Grill chicken and ribs until crisp and cooked through, brushing with marinade and turning occasionally, about 45 minutes.

Honey-Pecan Fried Chicken

6 to 8 servings

2 2½- to 3-pound frying chickens, cut into serving pieces
4 cups buttermilk

1 cup self-rising flour
¾ teaspoon salt
¼ teaspoon garlic powder
¼ teaspoon cayenne pepper

1 cup (2 sticks) butter
½ cup honey
½ cup coarsely chopped pecans

Vegetable oil (for frying)

Wash chicken pieces; pat dry. Pour buttermilk into large bowl. Add chicken. Cover and refrigerate 1½ hours.

Drain chicken. Combine flour, salt, garlic powder and cayenne. Dredge chicken in flour, shaking off excess. Let chicken stand 20 minutes at room temperature.

Melt butter in heavy small saucepan over low heat. Stir in honey and bring to boil. Add pecans and simmer glaze 15 minutes.

Meanwhile, heat ½ to ¾ inch oil in heavy large skillet to 375°F. Add chicken (in batches; do not crowd) and fry until crisp, golden brown and cooked through, about 7 minutes per side. Drain on paper towels. Arrange on platter. Pour glaze over. Serve fried chicken immediately.

Szechwan Fried Chicken

4 servings

1 3-pound frying chicken	6 cups vegetable oil
2¾ teaspoons coarse salt	1 cup all purpose flour
2½ teaspoons Szechwan peppercorn powder*	¼ teaspoon salt
2 teaspoons five-spice powder*	6 cilantro sprigs
3 ⅛-inch-thick slices ginger	1 lime, thinly sliced
2 green onions, trimmed	1 orange, thinly sliced

Pat chicken dry. Set breast side up on surface. Cover with towel. Press down on breast area until breastbone is cracked and flattened. Twist both hip/thigh sockets until joints are dislocated; do not tear skin. (Chicken should be flat and in one piece.) Mix coarse salt, 2¼ teaspoons peppercorn powder and five-spice powder. Rub half of mixture onto chicken. Rub remainder in cavity. Place ginger and green onions in cavity. Cover chicken and let stand 2 hours.

Set chicken on pie plate. Place plate on rack in steamer. Cover and steam over high heat 30 minutes. Remove green onions and ginger. Let steamed chicken cool to room temperature.

Heat oil in wok to 350°F. Drain liquid from chicken. Using cleaver, halve chicken lengthwise. Dredge in flour, shaking off excess. Slide half of chicken down side of wok into oil and fry until golden brown, about 3 minutes per side. Remove and drain on paper towels. Repeat with remaining chicken half. Cool slightly.

Separate wings from body. Cut off wing tips. Cut thighs crosswise into 4 pieces. Halve remaining chicken. Cut crosswise into 1½x2-inch pieces. Arrange on platter. Combine remaining ¼ teaspoon peppercorn powder and salt. Sprinkle over chicken. Garnish with cilantro and citrus rounds.

*Available at oriental markets.

Peanut Butter Chicken

Serve this African-style main course with rice, fried bananas and cold beer.

4 to 6 servings

½ cup peanut oil	¼ teaspoon cayenne pepper
1 3½-pound chicken, cut into 8 pieces	Salt
2 cups chopped onions	2 cups water
½ cup creamy peanut butter	Chopped peanuts

Heat oil in heavy large skillet over medium-high heat. Add chicken and cook until browned and tender, turning occasionally, about 25 minutes. Transfer chicken to platter. Pour off all but 2 tablespoons drippings. Add onions to same skillet and cook until soft, about 5 minutes. Stir in peanut butter, cayenne pepper and salt. Gradually mix in water. Return chicken to pan. Simmer until sauce thickens slightly. Transfer to serving platter. Garnish with chopped peanuts. Serve immediately.

Chicken in Beer

4 to 6 servings

½ cup all purpose flour
1 teaspoon salt
¼ teaspoon freshly ground pepper
1 3- to 3½-pound fryer, cut up
3 to 4 tablespoons butter

1 onion, thinly sliced
1½ cups beer, room temperature
½ cup whipping cream
2 tablespoons chopped fresh parsley

Combine flour, salt and pepper in shallow dish. Roll chicken pieces in flour, coating well. Melt butter in large skillet over medium-high heat. Add onion and chicken and cook, turning frequently, until chicken is golden, about 12 to 15 minutes. Add beer. Cover, reduce heat and simmer, turning occasionally, until chicken is tender, about 40 minutes. Blend in whipping cream and parsley. Increase heat to medium-high. Continue to cook until heated through, about 2 to 3 minutes. Transfer chicken to platter. Whisk sauce and pour over chicken. Serve immediately.

Chicken and Pork Adobo

Serve this hearty stew with rice and a green salad.

6 servings

2½ pounds chicken legs and thighs
1½ pounds lean boneless pork, cut into 1-inch cubes
¾ cup red wine vinegar
¾ cup water
¼ cup soy sauce
8 whole peppercorns

4 garlic cloves, minced (about 1 tablespoon)
1 bay leaf

2 tablespoons vegetable oil

Minced fresh parsley (garnish)

Arrange chicken and pork in shallow 9x13-inch baking dish. Combine vinegar, water, soy sauce, peppercorns, garlic and bay leaf in medium bowl and blend well. Pour over meat. Cover dish and refrigerate 1 hour, turning chicken and pork occasionally.

Remove chicken and pork from marinade using slotted spoon and set marinade aside. Pat meat dry. Heat oil in heavy Dutch oven or flameproof casserole (not cast iron) over medium-high heat. Add chicken in batches and brown well on all sides. Remove from pot. Add pork to same pan and brown well, adding more oil if necessary. Pour reserved marinade over pork. Bring to boil. Reduce heat, cover and simmer 15 minutes. Return chicken to pot. Cover and simmer until chicken and pork are tender, about 30 minutes more. Transfer to serving platter. Cover and keep warm.

Skim any fat from sauce. Boil over high heat until reduced to about ¾ cup. Spoon over chicken and pork. Garnish with parsley and serve.

Chicken Stew with Fennel and Pernod

8 servings

3 tablespoons olive oil
2 2½- to 3-pound chickens, cut up (do not use backs or wings)
3 cups chicken stock

3 tablespoons butter
4 carrots, minced
2 celery stalks, minced
2 garlic cloves, minced

½ cup minced fennel bulb
2 leeks, carefully washed and minced
5 tomatoes, peeled, seeded and diced
¼ teaspoon ground saffron

½ cup fresh basil, chopped
1 tablespoon Pernod
Salt and freshly ground pepper
½ cup (1 stick) butter (optional)

Heat oil in heavy large skillet over medium-high heat. Add chicken and sauté until golden. Remove breast pieces. Pour chicken broth into skillet and bring to simmer. Cover and cook 15 minutes. Return breast pieces to skillet and continue cooking until all chicken is done, about 20 more minutes. Transfer chicken to platter and set aside to cool. Skim fat from broth.

Heat butter in another large skillet over low heat. Add carrot, celery, garlic, fennel and leek. Cover and cook about 10 minutes. Increase heat to medium-high. Add tomatoes and cook, stirring constantly, until most of tomato liquid has evaporated. Dissolve saffron in about ¼ cup broth. Stir into vegetables, blending thoroughly.

Skin and bone chicken. Cut meat into bite-size pieces. Bring chicken broth to boil. Stir in chicken, vegetable mixture, chopped basil and liqueur. Season with salt and pepper to taste. Ladle into tureen or individual bowls. *(If desired, stew can be enriched at this point by stirring 1 tablespoon butter into each serving.)*

Chicken Baked with Fresh Tarragon Pesto

2 to 4 servings; can be doubled

4 green onions (white and light green parts), cut into 1-inch pieces
4 large garlic cloves
½ cup packed fresh Italian parsley leaves
¼ cup fresh tarragon or basil leaves
2 tablespoons walnut pieces

1½ teaspoons grated lemon peel
⅓ cup olive oil

Salt and freshly ground pepper

1 3½-pound chicken, cut into 4 pieces

Preheat oven to 450°F. Finely mince first 6 ingredients in processor. With machine running, add oil through feed tube and process to coarse paste. Season with salt and freshly ground pepper.

Grease baking dish. Pat chicken dry and arrange in dish. Spread pesto over chicken, coating all sides. Bake until tender, basting once, about 30 minutes for white meat and 35 minutes for dark meat. Serve with rice pilaf.

Baked Honey Chicken

4 servings

1 3-pound chicken, cut up
3 tablespoons finely chopped onion
2 tablespoons honey
2 tablespoons dark soy sauce
1 tablespoon minced fresh ginger
1 teaspoon minced garlic

¼ cup thinly sliced green onion, green part only

Arrange chicken in 9x13-inch baking dish. Combine onion, honey, soy sauce, ginger and garlic in small bowl and spoon over chicken. Marinate for 1 hour, turning once.

Preheat oven to 425°F. Bake chicken 30 minutes. Turn pieces over and sprinkle with green onion. Continue baking until chicken is tender, about 10 to 15 minutes. Serve immediately.

Sautéed Veal Scallops with Creamy Scrambled Eggs;
sweet raisin braid (recipe not included)

Irwin Horowitz

Honey-Pecan Fried Chicken

André Gillardin

Curried Turkey Salad

Dick Sharpe

Clockwise from top left: Fillet of Sole Stuffed with Shrimp; Red Snapper with Citrus; Shrimp in Green Sauce; Swordfish Indian Style

Irwin Horowitz

Rio Grande Fajitas

Peter A. Högg

*Fettuccine with Snow Peas,
Ham and Tomato*

Dick Sharpe

Brian Leatart

Curry-glazed Chicken

4 servings

2 tablespoons (¼ stick) butter
¼ cup honey
3 tablespoons Dijon mustard

2 teaspoons curry powder
½ teaspoon salt
1 2½-pound chicken, cut into pieces

Preheat oven to 375°F. Place butter in 9x13-inch baking dish and heat in oven until melted. Stir in honey, mustard, curry powder and salt. Add chicken, turning to coat. Bake 20 minutes. Turn chicken over. Continue baking until golden brown, 20 to 25 minutes. Serve hot.

Baked Chicken Kapama

An intriguing blend of spices—including oregano, cloves, allspice, cinnamon and chilies—flavors the tomato sauce for this traditional Greek dish.

12 servings

3 2- to 2½-pound frying chickens, quartered
¾ cup fresh lemon juice
Salt and freshly ground pepper

½ cup olive oil
2 tablespoons (¼ stick) butter
2 small dried red chilies
1 tablespoon ground allspice
1 teaspoon dried oregano, crumbled

1 small cinnamon stick
6 peppercorns
3 whole cloves
2 1½-pound cans whole tomatoes, drained and chopped
1 cup water
½ cup Retsina or other dry white wine
¼ cup tomato paste

Arrange chicken in single layer in baking dish. Cover with lemon juice, salt and pepper. Let stand at room temperature 1 hour, turning occasionally.

Heat oil with butter in heavy large skillet over medium-high heat. Drain chicken and pat dry. Brown in batches. Return to baking dish. Tie all spices in cheesecloth. Stir tomatoes, water, wine and tomato paste into same skillet, scraping up brown bits. Add spice bag. Reduce heat to medium and cook until sauce thickens, stirring occasionally, about 40 minutes.

Preheat oven to 350°F. Pour tomato mixture over chicken. Cover with foil. Bake until chicken is tender, about 40 minutes. Discard spice bag and serve.

Baked Chicken German Style

4 servings

¼ cup (½ stick) butter
5 tablespoons all purpose flour
1¼ cups chicken stock
⅔ cup milk
½ teaspoon fresh lemon juice
Salt and freshly ground pepper
Freshly grated nutmeg

1 pound egg noodles, freshly cooked
1 4-pound chicken, poached, cut into 8 pieces and skinned
⅔ cup freshly grated Parmesan cheese mixed with 1 teaspoon sweet paprika

Melt butter in heavy medium saucepan over medium-low heat. Whisk in flour and stir 3 minutes. Gradually whisk in 1 cup stock and milk. Increase heat and bring to boil. Reduce heat and simmer until thick, about 10 minutes. Blend in lemon juice. Season sauce with salt, pepper and nutmeg.

Preheat oven to 350°F. Moisten bottoms of 4 individual casseroles with remaining ¼ cup chicken broth. Layer each with noodles, 2 pieces of chicken and sauce. Top with cheese mixture. Bake until bubbling and golden brown, about 30 minutes. Serve immediately.

New Year's Chicken

6 servings

1 10-ounce package frozen puff pastry shells, partially thawed

¼ cup corn oil

3 whole chicken breasts, skinned, boned and split

Salt and freshly ground pepper

8 ounces *whipped* cream cheese with chives

On lightly floured surface roll out each pastry shell into 7- to 9-inch circle. Set aside.

Heat oil in large skillet over medium-high heat. Season chicken with salt and pepper. Add to skillet and fry on both sides until chicken is golden, 5 to 7 minutes. Drain chicken well.

Preheat oven to 450°F. Lightly grease baking sheet. Place a chicken breast on one half of each pastry circle. Spread 2 to 3 tablespoons of cream cheese over top of each piece. Fold remaining half of pastry over chicken, pressing edges to seal. Transfer to baking sheet. Reduce oven temperature to 400°F. Bake until pastry is puffed and golden, about 25 to 30 minutes. Serve hot.

Roast Chicken with Garlic Croutons

4 servings

1 3-pound chicken, neck and giblets reserved
Salt and freshly ground pepper

5½ ounces day-old French bread, cut into 1½x1½-inch croutons

3 large garlic cloves, halved

2 to 3 fresh thyme sprigs or ½ teaspoon dried, crumbled

2 tablespoons (¼ stick) butter

1 tablespoon vegetable oil
Fresh thyme sprigs

Pat chicken dry. Sprinkle cavity with salt and pepper. Rub croutons on all sides with garlic. Place 2 to 3 croutons and thyme in cavity. Truss chicken to hold shape. Sprinkle outside with salt and freshly ground pepper.

Position rack in center of oven and preheat to 375°F. Melt butter with oil in roasting pan over medium-high heat. Add chicken and brown well on all sides. Set chicken breast side up and roast 24 minutes. Add remaining croutons, neck and giblets to pan and roast until juices run clear when thigh is pierced with fork, about 12 minutes. Transfer to platter. Garnish with thyme. Pass croutons separately.

Garlic and Rosemary Roast Chicken

Serve this chicken fresh from the oven or pack it up for a picnic and enjoy it at room temperature.

2 to 4 servings

1 3½- to 4-pound chicken
Salt and freshly ground pepper

2 medium garlic cloves, flattened

3 fresh rosemary sprigs or 1 tablespoon dried, crumbled

¼ lemon
Paprika

3 tablespoons butter

3 tablespoons olive oil

6 ounces small shallots (about 9)

2 medium garlic cloves

1½ tablespoons fresh lemon juice

1 teaspoon minced fresh rosemary or ½ teaspoon dried, crumbled

1 large or 2 small red bell peppers, cored, seeded and cut into ¾x1½-inch pieces

¼ cup golden raisins

Preheat oven to 400°F. Pat chicken dry. Sprinkle inside and out with salt and pepper. Rub inside and out with flattened garlic and rosemary sprigs. Place 1 inch of rosemary sprig under skin over each side of breast. Place flattened garlic, remaining rosemary sprigs and lemon quarter in cavity. Truss chicken. Sprinkle with paprika.

Melt butter with oil in heavy large ovenproof skillet over high heat. Add chicken to skillet breast side up; add shallots and 2 whole garlic cloves. Cook until bottom of chicken is lightly browned, stirring vegetables frequently, about 4 minutes. Add lemon juice to skillet. Baste chicken with pan juices. Sprinkle vegetables with rosemary and season with salt and pepper.

Transfer skillet to oven and roast chicken 45 minutes, basting chicken and stirring vegetables occasionally. Mix bell peppers into skillet. Continue cooking, basting chicken and stirring vegetables occasionally, until juices run clear when chicken is pierced in thickest part of thigh, about 35 minutes, transferring shallots and garlic to strainer when very tender and deep golden brown. Transfer chicken to platter. Add peppers to shallots using slotted spoon. Place skillet with pan juices on top of stove. Add raisins and simmer 3 minutes to plump. Add to vegetables using slotted spoon. Serve chicken warm or at room temperature. Pass vegetables separately.

Carry's Chicken Livers with Apple

4 servings

2 to 3 tablespoons butter
1 large Spanish onion, diced
1 pound chicken livers
2 medium McIntosh apples, peeled, cored and chopped
Salt and freshly ground pepper

Freshly cooked rice
6 slices bacon, crisply cooked and crumbled

Heat butter in large skillet over medium-high heat. Add onion and sauté until translucent, about 5 minutes. Add chicken livers and sauté 2 minutes. Reduce heat to medium-low and cook until livers are slightly pink in centers, 4 to 5 minutes. Stir in chopped apple. Cover and cook 1 minute. Season with salt and pepper.

To serve, spoon over rice. Sprinkle with crumbled bacon and serve.

Chicken Livers Arroyo Perdido

8 servings

½ cup (1 stick) butter
2 pounds chicken livers
1 garlic clove, crushed
2 tablespoons potato flour
1 cup dry Rosé of Cabernet Sauvignon or other dry rosé

2 teaspoons red currant jelly
Salt and freshly ground pepper

20 freshly cooked scrambled eggs
Chopped fresh parsley

Melt ¼ cup butter in heavy medium skillet over medium-high heat. Add livers and sauté until light brown, about 2 minutes. Spoon livers and juices into dish. Melt remaining butter in same skillet over medium-high heat. Add garlic and sauté 30 seconds. Add flour and stir 1 minute. Remove pan from heat. Mix in wine and jelly. Set pan over medium heat and cook sauce until thickened, about 2 minutes. Season with salt and freshly ground pepper. Add chicken livers and simmer until cooked to desired doneness, about 7 minutes for rare.

Spoon scrambled eggs onto plate, leaving well in center. Spoon livers into center. Garnish with parsley. Serve immediately.

Turkey Hash with Sweet Potatoes and Turnips

Purchase a roasted turkey leg or whole chicken at your market. This is also a great use for leftover turkey.

2 servings; can be doubled or tripled

2 cups ½-inch dice skinned roasted turkey or chicken, bones reserved
3 cups unsalted chicken stock
1 bay leaf
1 8-ounce sweet potato, peeled and quartered lengthwise
½ pound turnips, peeled and quartered

2 tablespoons (¼ stick) butter
2 large onions, chopped

4 ounces mushrooms, quartered
¼ cup whipping cream
1 egg yolk
1 teaspoon minced fresh tarragon or ½ teaspoon dried, crumbled
Salt and freshly ground pepper
Minced fresh tarragon or dried, crumbled

Combine turkey bones, stock and bay leaf in large saucepan. Bring to boil. Add potato and turnips. Reduce heat, cover and simmer until vegetables are almost tender, about 12 minutes. Remove vegetables using slotted spoon. Simmer broth until reduced to 1½ cups, about 15 minutes. Strain. Cut vegetables into ½-inch dice.

Melt butter in heavy large skillet over medium-low heat. Add onions and cook until golden brown, stirring occasionally, about 10 minutes. Increase heat to high and add mushrooms, turnips and potato. Cook until vegetables are golden brown, stirring frequently, about 4 minutes. Add chicken broth and boil until slightly syrupy, about 5 minutes. Mix in turkey and stir to heat through. Remove from heat. Combine cream and yolk. Add to turkey. Mix in 1 teaspoon tarragon. Place over low heat and stir until sauce thickens, about 30 seconds; do not boil. Season with salt and pepper. Sprinkle with minced tarragon and serve.

Crisp Turkey Paillards with Capers

4 servings

1¼ pounds ¼-inch-thick turkey breast slices (about 8)
1 large lemon

2 eggs
Salt and freshly ground pepper
⅓ cup all purpose flour
¾ cup unseasoned dry breadcrumbs

3 tablespoons unsalted butter
3 tablespoons vegetable oil

¼ cup (½ stick) unsalted butter
¼ cup capers, drained
2 tablespoons minced fresh parsley
Lemon wedges

If necessary, pound each turkey slice between 2 sheets of plastic wrap to thickness of ¼ inch, using flat meat pounder or rolling pin. Cut peel and white pith from lemon. Cut between membranes of lemon with small sharp knife to release segments. Discard membranes and any seeds. Cut lemon into ¼-inch dice. *(Can be prepared 4 hours ahead. Cover and refrigerate. Bring to room temperature before continuing.)*

Preheat oven to 275°F. Beat eggs in shallow bowl. Sprinkle turkey with salt and pepper. Dust 1 slice with flour, shaking to remove excess. Dip in egg, then breadcrumbs, coating completely; pat and press lightly so crumbs adhere. Transfer to tray or large platter. Repeat with remaining slices, arranging in single layer.

Melt 3 tablespoons butter with oil in heavy large skillet over medium-high heat. Add turkey in batches (do not crowd) and cook until golden brown, about 1 minute per side. Arrange turkey in single layer on ovenproof platter and keep warm in oven.

Lightly brown ¼ cup butter in heavy medium saucepan over medium-low heat, shaking pan frequently. Sprinkle turkey with capers, parsley and lemon dice. Pour butter over turkey. Garnish with lemon wedges and serve.

5 🍃 Seafood

For truly easy, fresh cooking, fish and shellfish are a perfect choice. They need only brief cooking, and they blend beautifully with fresh vegetables, pasta and grains to make a quick, healthful meal. Although they taste good alone, simply broiled or grilled, they are even better when complemented with a light marinade or sauce.

Buy whatever is good and fresh at the market, and you will have the ingredients for an excellent fish dinner, such as Red Snapper with Citrus (page 97), quick-cooked fillets with orange and grapefruit juice and fruit; Lime-marinated Swordfish with Cilantro Butter (page 101), grilled steaks in a tangy butter sauce; or Spiced Pan-fried Trout (page 102), sautéed whole fish in a spicy cornmeal coating. With a little advance planning, you can have dinner party entrées that require only a few minutes' finishing just before serving, such as thinly sliced Fillet of Sole with Fresh Ginger (page 94) and Shark with Cilantro and Sour Cream Sauce (page 100).

The wonderful thing about shellfish is that they mix so well with other ingredients. With their rich textures and flavors, a little shellfish usually goes a long way, so they are also an economical addition to a stew or salad. And served on their own, they provide a delicious canvas for an array of colorful sauces and accompaniments. Shrimp, salmon and scallops come together with green vegetables and herbs for a flavorful Summer Seafood Blanquette with Chard and Snow Peas (page 104); Steamed Clams and Mussels with Italian Sausage (page 113) makes a hearty Mediterranean stew; for summer parties, Hickory-barbecued Shrimp (page 105), with its garlic dipping sauce, is a natural; and Wild Rice and Shrimp Casserole (page 110), prepared in the microwave, is great for a weeknight supper. Whether you try the down-home Seafood Jambalaya (page 105) or elegant Coquilles Saint-Jacques with Zucchini Mousse (page 112), these easy recipes bring a whole new definition to the term "fast food."

Fish

Fish Fillets Dijon

4 to 6 servings

8 fish fillets (about 2 pounds total)
2 tablespoons Dijon mustard
¾ cup fine dry breadcrumbs
½ teaspoon seasoned salt
¼ teaspoon dried thyme, crumbled
⅛ teaspoon freshly ground pepper

3 to 4 tablespoons bottled Italian
   salad dressing or vinaigrette
8 tablespoons (1 stick) butter
8 lemon wedges
   Chopped fresh parsley (garnish)

Preheat oven to 450°F. Arrange fish fillets in single layer in shallow pan. Spread mustard evenly over fillets. Combine breadcrumbs, salt, thyme and pepper in small bowl. Sprinkle breadcrumb mixture evenly over fillets. Drizzle salad dressing over crumbs. Bake fillets until tender, about 5 to 7 minutes. Dot each with 1 tablespoon butter and top with lemon wedge. Garnish with parsley.

Fillet of Sole with Fresh Ginger

2 servings

¾ to 1 pound skinned sole fillets
   Melted butter
   Coarse salt
   Freshly ground white pepper

Fresh Ginger Sauce
¾ cup water
½ cup julienne of peeled fresh ginger
⅓ cup sugar
1 cup dry white wine

5 tablespoons unsalted butter, cut
   into ½-inch pieces
1½ teaspoons fresh lemon juice
   Coarse salt and freshly ground
   white pepper

6 small melon balls (garnish)
2 mint sprigs (garnish)

Cut fish according to instructions (see page 48). Lightly brush 2 ovenproof plates with melted butter and sprinkle lightly with salt and white pepper. Arrange fish in center of each plate. Brush lightly with butter and sprinkle with salt and pepper. Press small piece of waxed paper on top of fish. Set plates aside while preparing sauce.

For sauce: Combine water, ginger and sugar in heavy 2-quart saucepan. Place over medium-low heat and stir until sugar is dissolved. Cover and continue cooking 30 minutes. Uncover, increase heat and cook until liquid is reduced to about ¼ cup. Add wine and continue cooking until liquid is reduced to ¼ cup. Remove sauce from heat and discard about half of ginger.

Preheat oven to 450°F. Whisk butter into sauce 1 piece at a time, making sure each piece is fully incorporated before adding the next (return pan to low heat if necessary). Stir in lemon juice, salt and white pepper. Set aside and keep warm.

Bake fish 3 minutes. Remove plates from oven and let stand 30 seconds. Discard waxed paper. Spoon sauce over each piece of fish. Place melon balls and mint sprigs on left side of each plate and serve.

Fillet of Sole Pesto

4 servings

2 tablespoons (¼ stick) butter
3 medium tomatoes, peeled, seeded and chopped
3 tablespoons chopped fresh parsley

1 pound sole fillets, patted dry
⅓ to ½ cup Pesto Mayonnaise*

Additional Pesto Mayonnaise

Preheat oven to 350°F. Melt butter in large ovenproof skillet. Remove from heat. Add tomatoes and parsley and toss to coat with butter. Arrange fillets over top without overlapping. Spread with ⅓ to ½ cup Pesto Mayonnaise. Cover skillet tightly with foil. Bake just until fish is cooked through, 5 to 8 minutes; do not overcook.

Discard foil. Transfer fish and tomato mixture to heated platter using slotted spoon (reserve juices for another use if desired). Serve immediately with additional Pesto Mayonnaise.

*Pesto Mayonnaise

This also makes an excellent dressing for potato, pasta, chicken, fish and beef salads.

Makes about 1¾ cups

2 egg yolks, room temperature
2 garlic cloves, halved
1 tablespoon garlic vinegar
1½ cups firmly packed fresh basil leaves

2 fresh spinach leaves, stemmed
1 cup vegetable oil
¾ teaspoon salt or to taste

Mix yolks, garlic and vinegar in processor or blender. Blend in basil and spinach. With machine running, add oil in slow, steady stream, blending until mayonnaise is smooth and thick. Season with salt to taste.

Sole in Mustard Cream

4 servings

2 tablespoons (¼ stick) butter
1½ tablespoons diced onion
2 tablespoons red wine vinegar
¾ cup whipping cream

1 pound sole fillets
1½ tablespoons Dijon mustard
Freshly cooked rice

Melt butter in heavy large skillet over medium-low heat. Add onion and sauté until very soft, 10 to 15 minutes. Increase heat to medium-high. Add vinegar and boil until almost evaporated, about 2 minutes. Add cream and boil until reduced by half, about 5 minutes. Add fish and cook until opaque, turning once, about 5 minutes. Gently remove fish; keep warm. Add mustard to skillet and heat briefly; do not boil. Return fish to skillet and spoon sauce over. Serve immediately over rice.

Breaded Sole Fillets with Parsley-Lemon Butter

4 servings

Parsley-Lemon Butter
9 tablespoons unsalted butter, room temperature
2¼ teaspoons strained fresh lemon juice
2¼ tablespoons minced fresh parsley
Salt and freshly ground pepper

¾ cup fine fresh breadcrumbs
1½ pounds ¼-inch-thick sole fillets
2 eggs blended with 2 tablespoons milk
Salt and freshly ground pepper

6 tablespoons clarified butter

For butter: Beat 9 tablespoons butter until smooth, using wooden spoon. Gradually mix in lemon juice. Stir in parsley, salt and pepper. *(Can be prepared 2 days ahead and refrigerated. Bring to room temperature before using.)*

Spread breadcrumbs on large plate. Dip each fillet in egg mixture, then coat both sides with breadcrumbs, pressing gently. Arrange in single layer on another large plate. Sprinkle both sides with salt and pepper.

Heat clarified butter in heavy large skillet over medium-high heat. Cook fish in batches (do not crowd) until golden brown, reducing heat if butter browns, about 1 minute per side. Arrange in single layer on heated platter and keep warm in 200°F oven while cooking remaining fish. Top each with some of parsley butter. Serve immediately, passing remaining parsley butter.

Fillet of Sole Stuffed with Shrimp

6 servings

6 ounces cooked shrimp
6 ounces feta cheese, room temperature
2 tablespoons water
2 cups finely chopped spinach
3 green onions, tops only, chopped
6 water chestnuts, chopped

6 4-ounce fresh sole fillets
Freshly ground pepper
¼ cup dry white wine

6 ½-inch-thick tomato slices
Salt
6 basil or watercress leaves

Set aside 3 shrimp. Chop remainder. Crumble cheese into bowl. Blend in water. Add chopped shrimp, spinach, ¾ of onion tops and water chestnuts.

Preheat oven to 325°F. Pat sole dry. Set on work surface. Sprinkle with pepper. Divide shrimp mixture among fillets, spreading evenly. Starting at short end, roll up fillets; secure with toothpicks. Arrange in baking dish. Pour wine into dish. Cover and bake until sole is opaque and filling is heated through, 15 to 20 minutes.

Meanwhile, arrange tomatoes on baking sheet. Sprinkle with salt and pepper. Set basil or watercress leaf on each tomato. Bake 15 minutes.

Transfer sole and tomatoes to plates. Slice reserved shrimp in half. Top each portion with shrimp half. Sprinkle with remaining onions. Serve immediately.

Sole-stuffed Potatoes

4 servings

4 large baking potatoes (about ½ pound each), scrubbed and dried

1 medium onion, finely chopped
1½ tablespoons light vegetable oil (preferably cold-pressed safflower) or unsalted butter
1 teaspoon potato flour or cornstarch
2 large ripe tomatoes, peeled, seeded and cut julienne (about 2 cups)
2 tablespoons tomato paste

1 teaspoon tamari soy sauce
Cayenne pepper
1 tablespoon finely chopped parsley
1 tablespoon chopped chives
Herb or vegetable salt (optional)
4 small fillets of sole (or 2 large fillets, halved), rolled and secured with toothpicks

1 to 2 tablespoons skim milk
8 watercress sprigs (garnish)

Position rack in top third of oven and preheat to 425°F. Pierce potato skins. Bake potatoes until tender, about 1 hour. Cut thin slice off top of each potato. Carefully scoop potato pulp from shells, leaving thin layer of pulp around sides. Set aside.

Combine onion and ½ tablespoon oil in medium saucepan. Cook over low heat, stirring constantly, until onion is soft and translucent. Remove from heat. Add potato flour and stir until combined. Add tomato julienne, tomato paste, soy sauce and cayenne pepper to taste. Cook over medium heat, stirring constantly, until tomatoes render juices, about 5 to 10 minutes. Add parsley and chives. Season with herb salt to taste. Reduce heat to low, add sole and continue cooking until fish just turns opaque, about 4 to 5 minutes. Remove fillets with slotted spoon. Arrange in reserved potato shells. Cover each fillet with about 1 tablespoon tomato sauce.

Preheat broiler. Transfer potato pulp to large bowl of electric mixer and beat until smooth. Add remaining 1 tablespoon oil and mix well. If puree is too stiff to pipe through pastry bag, add 1 to 2 tablespoons milk. Transfer puree to pastry bag fitted with large star tip and pipe rosettes or ribbons atop fillets (or spoon puree over). Broil until tops are brown. Garnish with watercress. Serve with remaining tomato sauce.

Red Snapper with Citrus

4 servings

1 grapefruit
1 orange

½ cup fresh orange juice
½ cup fresh grapefruit juice
1 large garlic clove, pressed

¼ teaspoon dried thyme, crushed
¼ teaspoon salt
Freshly ground pepper
4 6-ounce red snapper fillets
¼ cup minced fresh parsley

Using small sharp knife, remove colored part of peel from half of grapefruit and orange. Cut into matchstick julienne. Blanch in boiling water 10 minutes. Drain; rinse under cold water. Section grapefruit.

Bring juices, garlic, thyme, salt and pepper to boil in large nonstick skillet. Add fish and cover loosely. Reduce heat and simmer until just opaque, about 5 minutes, turning once. Transfer fish to platter. Boil liquid in skillet until reduced to thin sauce-like consistency. Pour over fish. Garnish with grapefruit sections, citrus julienne and parsley. Serve immediately.

Red Snapper Sautéed with Shallots and Pistachios

4 servings

1 cup dry white wine
3 tablespoons minced shallots
2½ tablespoons strained fresh lime juice
2 teaspoons minced garlic
12 tablespoons (1½ sticks) well-chilled unsalted butter, cut into 12 pieces

½ cup chopped unsalted pistachios
1½ teaspoons minced fresh parsley
Salt and freshly ground pepper

4 8-ounce red snapper fillets
¾ cup all purpose flour
6 tablespoons olive oil

Boil wine with shallots in heavy small saucepan until reduced by ⅓. Add lime juice and garlic and boil 30 seconds. Remove from heat and whisk in 2 tablespoons butter. Set pan over low heat and whisk in remaining butter 1 tablespoon at a time, removing pan from heat briefly if drops of melted butter appear. (If sauce breaks down at any time, remove from heat and whisk in 2 tablespoons cold butter. Return to low heat and whisk in remaining butter.) Add nuts and parsley. Season with salt and pepper. Keep warm in water bath.

Dredge fish in flour, shaking off excess. Heat oil in heavy large skillet over medium-high heat. Add fish (in batches if necessary; do not crowd) and brown well, 3 to 4 minutes per side. Transfer to platter. Spoon sauce over. Serve immediately.

Grilled Salmon with Lime Cream Sauce

*A simple-to-prepare entrée
that showcases the fresh
flavor of salmon.*

6 servings

3 cups whipping cream
2½ teaspoons lime peel julienne

6 6-ounce salmon fillets (1 inch
    thick)
    Melted butter

Salt and freshly ground white
pepper

1 tablespoon fresh lime juice
    Watercress

Boil whipping cream and 1½ teaspoons lime peel in heavy nonaluminum saucepan until reduced to 1½ cups.

Prepare barbecue grill (medium-high heat). Grease grill rack. Brush salmon with butter; sprinkle with salt and pepper. Arrange on rack. Cook until just opaque, basting with butter occasionally, about 4 minutes per side.

Transfer salmon to plates. Whisk lime juice and remaining 1 teaspoon lime peel into sauce. Season with salt and pepper. Spoon sauce over salmon. Garnish with watercress and serve.

Sautéed Salmon with Spinach and Red Bell Pepper Sauce

4 to 6 servings

1½ pounds salmon fillet, preferably
    from tail end

Red Pepper Sauce
  2 large red bell peppers, roasted and
    peeled
½ cup dry white wine
  6 tablespoons white wine vinegar
  4 thyme sprigs
    Salt and freshly ground pepper

1 cup (2 sticks) well-chilled unsalted
    butter, cut into tablespoons

2 tablespoons (¼ stick) unsalted
    butter
1½ pounds spinach, stemmed and
    cooked until tender

2 tablespoons vegetable oil

Using tweezers, remove small bones from salmon. Place salmon skin side down on surface. Cut salmon on diagonal into ½-inch-thick slices and remove from skin. Layer salmon between lightly oiled waxed paper and pound to thickness of ¼ inch.

For sauce: Halve bell peppers; pat dry. Puree in processor. Boil wine, vinegar and thyme in heavy medium saucepan until reduced to 3 tablespoons. Strain and return to saucepan. Add bell pepper puree and bring to boil. *(Can be prepared 1 day ahead. Cool completely, cover and refrigerate.)* Season with salt and pepper. Remove from heat and whisk in 2 tablespoons chilled butter. Set pan over low heat and whisk in remaining 14 tablespoons butter 1 tablespoon at a time, removing pan from heat briefly if drops of melted butter appear. (If sauce breaks down at any time, remove from heat and whisk in 2 tablespoons chilled butter.) Keep sauce warm on rack over hot water.

Melt 2 tablespoons butter in medium skillet over low heat. Add spinach and stir until heated through. Season with salt and freshly ground pepper.

Pat salmon dry. Sprinkle with salt and pepper. Heat oil in heavy large skillet over high heat. Add salmon in batches and sear quickly, 30 seconds per side.

Spoon some of sauce onto platter or plates. Top with salmon. Surround with spinach. Pass remaining sauce.

Salmon in Sorrel Sauce

2 servings

2 ½-pound salmon steaks

2 tablespoons (¼ stick) butter
2 shallots, finely minced
¾ cup dry white wine
1 cup chicken stock

2 cups whipping cream
6 tablespoons finely chopped sorrel leaves
Salt and freshly ground pepper

Preheat broiler. Broil salmon until opaque, about 4 minutes per side. Keep warm.

Melt butter in medium skillet over medium heat. Add shallots and sauté until tender, 1 to 2 minutes. Add wine, increase heat to high and boil until reduced to glaze, about 3 minutes. Add stock and boil until reduced to ⅓ cup, about 4 minutes. Reduce heat to medium. Stir in cream and sorrel. Cook until thickened, about 8 minutes. Season with salt and pepper. Serve salmon, passing sorrel sauce separately.

Piccata of Mako Shark

4 servings

4 ⅜-inch-thick slices mako
  or thresher shark (about
  3 ounces each)
  Salt and freshly ground pepper
  All purpose flour
½ cup (1 stick) butter

1 tablespoon capers, rinsed and
  drained
1 small lemon, peeled and separated
  into segments
  Chopped fresh parsley

Season shark with salt and pepper. Dredge in flour, shaking off excess. Melt ¼ cup butter in heavy large skillet over medium heat. Add shark and cook until browned, about 1 minute per side. Remove to heated serving platter. Wipe skillet clean; melt remaining butter. Add capers and lemon segments and sauté 2 minutes. Pour caper sauce over shark. Sprinkle with parsley and serve immediately.

Shark Steaks in Oyster Sauce

4 servings

4 1-inch-thick shark steaks (½ to
  ¾ pound each)
  Freshly ground pepper

1 tablespoon sesame oil
1 cup sliced mushrooms

½ cup diced green onion tops
1 small garlic clove, minced
½ cup oyster sauce
½ cup soy sauce
1 medium tomato, thinly sliced

Season fish with pepper. Place on elevated rack in Dutch oven or wok. Pour in enough water to come just below rack. Cover and bring to boil over high heat: Steam fish until tender, about 5 minutes, turning once.

Meanwhile, heat oil in large skillet over medium heat. Add mushrooms, onion and garlic and sauté until mushrooms release their liquid, 3 to 5 minutes. Stir in oyster and soy sauces. Add fish to skillet and cook 1 minute per side. Transfer fish to serving platter. Remove mushrooms using slotted spoon and mound atop fish. Garnish with tomato. Pass sauce separately.

Shark with Cilantro and Sour Cream Sauce

This spicy sauce perks up swordfish and halibut as well as shark.

4 servings

Cilantro and Sour Cream Sauce
- 2 large garlic cloves
- ½ jalapeño chili, seeded and quartered
- ¼ cup firmly packed parsley sprigs
- ¼ cup loosely packed cilantro leaves
  Salt
- 2 egg yolks, room temperature
- ¾ cup vegetable oil
- ½ cup sour cream

Shark
- 1½ pounds shark fillet (about 1 inch thick), cut into 4 pieces

- 3 tablespoons vegetable oil
- 2 teaspoons fresh lemon juice

- 8 large unshelled shrimp
  Salt and freshly ground pepper

- 2 teaspoons white wine vinegar
- 8 lettuce leaves
  Lemon wedges

For sauce: With processor running, drop garlic and chili through feed tube and mix to paste, stopping to scrape down sides of bowl. Add parsley, cilantro and pinch of salt and chop finely. Blend in yolks and 1 tablespoon oil. With machine running, add remaining oil through feed tube in thin stream and mix until sauce is thick and smooth, stopping to scrape down sides of bowl. Transfer to bowl. Stir in sour cream. Season with salt. Refrigerate until ready to use. *(Can be prepared 1 day ahead.)*

For shark: Arrange shark in shallow bowl. Sprinkle with 1 tablespoon oil and lemon juice. Let stand 30 minutes, turning shark twice.

Preheat broiler or grill. Broil shrimp 2 inches from heat source until shells turn bright pink, about 1½ minutes per side. Transfer to plate. Season shark with salt and pepper. Broil until opaque, about 3 minutes per side. Transfer to plate. Let cool to room temperature. Shell shrimp.

Gradually whisk remaining oil into vinegar. Season with salt and pepper. Add lettuce and toss well. Mound lettuce on platter or plates. Top with shark. Coat shark with sauce. Set shrimp atop shark. Garnish with lemon and serve immediately. Pass remaining sauce separately.

Swordfish Indian Style

6 servings

- 1 teaspoon whole coriander seeds
- ½ teaspoon whole white peppercorns
- ½ teaspoon ground cardamom
- ¼ teaspoon ground turmeric
- 8 ounces plain low-fat yogurt
- 1 teaspoon salt
- 1 teaspoon grated peeled ginger

- 2 pounds swordfish, cut into 6 pieces (about 1 inch thick)

- 1 medium ripe papaya, peeled and thinly sliced
- 1 lime, halved
- 6 cilantro sprigs
  Lime slices

Grind coriander, peppercorns, cardamom and turmeric to powder in spice grinder or mortar. Blend 1½ to 1¾ teaspoons mixture into yogurt. Stir in salt and grated ginger. Cover and refrigerate marinade overnight.

Spread fish with marinade on both sides. Let stand 30 minutes.

Preheat broiler. Wipe all but thin coating of marinade off fish. Arrange on broiler pan. Broil 5 inches from heat source 5 minutes per side. Transfer to plates. Arrange papaya on broiler pan. Squeeze lime juice over. Broil until papaya softens slightly, about 30 seconds per side. Surround fish with papaya. Garnish with cilantro and lime slices. Serve immediately.

Lime-marinated Swordfish with Cilantro Butter

4 servings

4 6-ounce 1-inch-thick swordfish steaks
2½ tablespoons lime juice
Salt and freshly ground pepper

½ cup (1 stick) butter

1 garlic clove, minced
¾ cup fresh cilantro, finely chopped
½ teaspoon dried red pepper flakes
Lime wedges

Place swordfish in nonaluminum dish. Pour lime juice over. Season with salt and pepper. Marinate 20 minutes, turning once.

Prepare barbecue (medium heat) or preheat broiler. Melt butter in heavy small saucepan over medium heat. Add garlic and cook 30 seconds. Mix in cilantro and pepper flakes and cook until cilantro is heated through, about 1 minute. Grill swordfish until just opaque, about 7 minutes per side, basting frequently with cilantro butter. Serve with lime wedges.

Swordfish Sukiyaki

2 servings; can be doubled or tripled

½ 6¾-ounce package rice sticks (noodles)
Boiling water

1 cup clam juice
6 tablespoons saké
¼ cup soy sauce
1 to 2 tablespoons sugar
2 tablespoons vegetable oil
2 bunches green onions (white and light green parts), halved lengthwise and cut into 1½-inch pieces

¾ pound swordfish, cut diagonally into ⅓-inch-thick slices
2 3.5-ounce packages enoki mushrooms, trimmed
¼ teaspoon minced fresh ginger
½ 14.2-ounce package Japanese tofu, cut into 2½x⅓-inch strips
1 bunch watercress, stemmed

Place rice sticks in large bowl. Add enough boiling water to cover. Let stand until softened, 15 minutes.

Meanwhile, combine clam juice, saké, soy sauce and sugar in small bowl; stir until sugar dissolves. Heat oil in heavy large skillet over high heat. Add green onions and stir until beginning to soften and just beginning to color, about 2 minutes. Add swordfish, mushrooms and ginger and stir 1 minute. Add clam juice mixture, then tofu and watercress. Simmer until fish is just cooked through, about 1 minute. Drain noodles and divide between bowls. Spoon fish mixture over.

Swordfish with Ginger, Leek and Garlic

This fish is delicate in flavor and easy to make.

6 servings

½ cup (1 stick) unsalted butter
3 medium leeks (white and light green parts), cut into ½-inch-thick rounds
4 medium garlic cloves, minced
1 1-inch piece peeled fresh ginger, grated on extra-fine grater* (discard fibers that stick to grater)

Salt and freshly ground white pepper

Olive oil
6 7-ounce swordfish, sturgeon or ono fillets (½-inch thick)
Fresh basil
Chive blossoms (optional)

Prepare barbecue grill (high heat).

Melt butter in heavy medium skillet over medium-low heat. Add leeks, garlic and ginger and cook until leeks are tender, stirring frequently, about 15 minutes. Season with salt and pepper. Cover mixture and keep warm.

Coat grill rack with olive oil. Sprinkle fish with salt and pepper; brush with olive oil. Arrange on grill rack and cook until just opaque, about 2½ minutes per side. Transfer fish to plates. Spoon leek mixture over. Garnish with basil and chive blossoms. Serve immediately.

*If an extra-fine grater is not available, grate fresh ginger and squeeze juice. Add juice to leeks, discarding ginger fibers.

Swordfish with Grapefruit and Rosemary Butter Sauce

2 servings; can be doubled or tripled

2 6-ounce swordfish steaks, 1 to 1¼ inches thick
Salt and freshly ground pepper
1 tablespoon butter

2 shallots, minced
1 teaspoon dried rosemary, crumbled

¾ cup fresh grapefruit juice
2 tablespoons (¼ stick) unsalted butter
Fresh parsley sprigs

Season fish with salt and pepper. Melt 1 tablespoon butter in heavy medium skillet over medium heat. Add fish and cook until just opaque, about 9 minutes per inch of thickness, turning once. Transfer fish to warm platter. Tent with foil to keep warm.

Pour off all but film of butter from skillet. Add shallots and rosemary and stir over medium heat until shallots soften, about 2 minutes. Add grapefruit juice. Increase heat and bring to boil, scraping up any browned bits. Add any juices from fish platter. Boil until sauce is syrupy, 5 to 8 minutes. Remove from heat and swirl in 2 tablespoons butter 1 tablespoon at a time. Season sauce with salt and pepper. Spoon over fish. Garnish with parsley.

Spiced Pan-fried Trout

2 servings; can be doubled or tripled

2 8- to 10-ounce boned and butterflied trout
1 cup milk

⅓ cup yellow cornmeal
2 tablespoons all purpose flour
½ teaspoon chili powder
½ teaspoon ground cumin
Salt and freshly ground pepper

4 tablespoons (½ stick) unsalted butter
2 tablespoons vegetable oil

½ teaspoon chili powder
½ teaspoon ground cumin
½ teaspoon salt
1 tablespoon fresh lemon juice
Minced fresh parsley

Open trout and arrange in shallow pan. Add milk and soak 20 minutes, turning trout occasionally.

Combine cornmeal, flour, ½ teaspoon chili powder and ½ teaspoon cumin in another shallow pan. Season generously with salt and pepper. Melt 2 tablespoons butter with oil in heavy large skillet over medium-high heat. Remove trout from milk and dip into cornmeal mixture, coating both sides completely. Add to skillet, skin side down. Cook until just opaque, about 1½ minutes per side. Transfer to serving plates; keep trout warm.

Pour off pan drippings and wipe out skillet; do not wash. Melt remaining 2 tablespoons butter in same skillet over medium-high heat. Add ½ teaspoon *each* chili powder, cumin and salt and stir 30 seconds. Stir in lemon juice (be careful; mixture will foam). Pour over trout. Sprinkle with parsley and serve.

Trout with Shrimp, Chives and Cream

4 servings

4 10- to 12-ounce trout, cleaned and scaled
⅓ cup all purpose flour
   Salt and freshly ground pepper

2 tablespoons (¼ stick) unsalted butter
3 tablespoons vegetable oil

Sauce
1 tablespoon unsalted butter
3 tablespoons minced shallot
¼ cup dry white wine
1 tablespoon white wine vinegar
1 cup whipping cream
¼ pound small shrimp, shelled
2 tablespoons snipped fresh chives

Trim fins and tails from trout using kitchen shears. If too long for large skillet, remove heads. Rinse fish inside and out, removing any flesh around backbones. Pat fish dry. Spread flour on large plate. Sprinkle fish inside and out with salt and pepper. Dip in flour to coat both sides, shaking off excess. Arrange on another large plate.

Melt 2 tablespoons butter with oil in heavy large skillet over medium heat. Cook 2 fish 4 minutes on first side, reducing heat to medium-low when browned. Turn fish, increase heat to medium and cook about 4 more minutes (thin skewer inserted in thickest part of fish for 10 seconds will be just hot when touched to inner wrist), reducing heat to medium-low when browned. Arrange on heated platter or large gratin dish and tent with foil. Repeat with remaining fish.

For sauce: Scrape up any browned bits on bottom of skillet and discard with fat. Melt butter in same skillet over low heat. Cook shallot until soft, stirring frequently, about 4 minutes. Pour in wine and vinegar, increase heat and boil until reduced to 1 tablespoon. Stir in cream. Season with salt and pepper. Boil until sauce coats back of wooden spoon, stirring frequently. Reduce heat to low and mix in shrimp. Simmer until just opaque, about 1 minute. Remove from heat and stir in chives. Adjust seasoning. Discard skin from top of fish. Set on platter. Pour sauce over and serve.

 *Shellfish*

Summer Seafood Blanquette with Chard and Snow Peas

For this colorful stew, sea bass can be substituted for the salmon.

4 servings

2 cups Simple Fish Stock*	½ pound Swiss chard, stemmed, halved lengthwise, cut crosswise into ½-inch strips and blanched 3 minutes
½ cup dry white wine	
8 jumbo shrimp, shelled and deveined, shells reserved	
1 cup whipping cream	½ pound snow peas, trimmed and blanched 1 minute
Salt and freshly ground pepper	1 tablespoon minced fresh tarragon
¾ pound salmon fillet, small bones removed, skinned and cut into 1-inch cubes	1 tablespoon snipped fresh chives
	1 tablespoon minced fresh parsley
¼ pound small sea scallops, trimmed	

Bring stock, wine and shells to boil in heavy medium saucepan. Reduce heat and simmer gently 15 minutes. Strain liquid into heavy large skillet; discard shells. Add half of cream and bring to simmer, stirring. Season with salt and pepper. Reduce heat to low. Add shrimp and cook 1 minute. Turn shrimp over. Add salmon and scallops and cook until just tender, about 4 minutes, shaking pan occasionally. Remove seafood using slotted spoon. Divide seafood among shallow bowls.

Boil sauce until reduced to 1 cup. Whisk in remaining cream and boil until sauce is thick enough to coat back of spoon, about 10 minutes. Stir in chard and peas and heat through. Remove from heat. Stir in herbs. Adjust seasoning. Pour off any liquid exuded from seafood. Transfer vegetables to bowls using slotted spoon. Pour sauce over. Serve immediately.

*Simple Fish Stock

Makes about 1 quart

1½ pounds bones, tails and heads from nonoily fish or 1 pound fish pieces for chowder	5 parsley stems
	1 bay leaf
	1 thyme sprig or pinch of dried, crumbled
1 tablespoon unsalted butter	
1 medium onion, sliced	

Rinse fish bones under cold running water at least 5 minutes.

Melt butter in large saucepan over low heat. Add onion and cook until softened, stirring occasionally, about 5 minutes. Add bones, remaining ingredients and water to cover. Bring to boil, skimming foam from surface. Reduce heat and simmer for 20 minutes, skimming occasionally. Strain through fine sieve without pressing on solids. Refrigerate until ready to use. *(Can be prepared 1 day ahead.)*

Seafood Jambalaya

4 to 6 servings

2 tablespoons (¼ stick) butter
2 large yellow onions, chopped
2 garlic cloves, chopped
2 28-ounce cans Italian plum tomatoes, drained (½ cup liquid reserved)
2½ cups chicken stock
1 medium green bell pepper, seeded and chopped
½ teaspoon dried thyme, crumbled

½ teaspoon dried red pepper flakes, crushed
1 bay leaf
Salt and freshly ground pepper
2 cups uncooked rice

1 pound large shrimp, peeled and deveined
1 pound sea scallops

Melt butter in Dutch oven over low heat. Add onions and garlic and stir until translucent, about 3 minutes. Add tomatoes with reserved liquid, stock, bell pepper, thyme, pepper flakes, bay leaf, salt and pepper. Bring to boil. Stir in rice. Cover and simmer until liquid is absorbed, about 30 minutes.

Add shrimp and scallops to rice mixture. Continue cooking until seafood is just opaque, about 2 minutes. Discard bay leaf. Taste and adjust seasoning.

Hickory-barbecued Shrimp

An easy-to-prepare entrée for summer parties. Guests can shell their own shrimp and dip them in a garlic sauce.

6 servings

1 cup (2 sticks) butter
3 bunches green onions (white part and 2 inches of green part), chopped
12 medium garlic cloves, chopped
1¾ cups dry white wine
2 tablespoons plus 1 teaspoon fresh lemon juice
Freshly ground pepper
36 large shrimp in shell, legs removed
1 cup minced fresh parsley

8 2-inch hickory chunks, soaked in water 15 minutes and drained

Hot pepper sauce
Salt

Lemon and lime wedges
2 tablespoons minced fresh parsley
2 tablespoons minced green onions
2 tablespoons snipped fresh chives

Melt butter in heavy Dutch oven over medium-low heat. Add 3 bunches green onions and garlic and stir 3 minutes. Add wine and simmer 15 minutes. Remove from heat and stir in lemon juice and generous amount of pepper. Cool. Cut shrimp down back and remove vein; do not peel. Add shrimp and 1 cup parsley to butter mixture. Refrigerate 6 hours or overnight, turning occasionally.

Prepare barbecue grill. When coals are gray, add hickory chunks and let heat until wood smokes, about 15 minutes.

Meanwhile, remove shrimp from marinade. Heat marinade in heavy medium saucepan. Strain and return to pan. Cook over medium-high heat until reduced by half, 5 to 10 minutes. Add hot pepper sauce and salt to taste. Cover and keep warm.

Place shrimp on grill rack and cook until just opaque, turning once, about 5 minutes. Mound shrimp on platter. Garnish with lemon and lime wedges. Pour sauce into ramekin(s) or serving bowl(s); sprinkle with minced parsley, green onions and chives. Serve shrimp and dipping sauce immediately.

Cajun Shrimp

8 servings

4 pounds medium shrimp, shelled and deveined
1 cup vegetable oil
½ cup chopped green onions
2 garlic cloves, minced
1 teaspoon cayenne pepper

1 teaspoon freshly ground pepper
½ teaspoon salt
½ teaspoon dried red pepper flakes
½ teaspoon dried thyme, crumbled
½ teaspoon dried rosemary, crumbled
¼ teaspoon dried oregano, crumbled

Combine all ingredients in large bowl, stirring to coat shrimp. Cover and refrigerate 2 hours, stirring occasionally. Soak bamboo skewers in water 2 hours and drain.

Prepare barbecue grill (medium-high heat). Position rack 4 to 6 inches from fire. Drain shrimp, reserving marinade. Thread shrimp on skewers. Grease barbecue rack. Place shrimp on rack and cook until just pink, basting with marinade, about 3 minutes per side. Serve immediately.

Sautéed Shrimp with Garlic and Herbs

4 to 6 servings

3 pounds large shrimp, peeled and deveined
⅓ cup olive oil

6 medium garlic cloves, blanched in boiling water 2 minutes, drained and finely minced
¾ cup dry white wine
1½ tablespoons fresh lemon juice

¾ cup (1½ sticks) unsalted butter, cut into ½-inch pieces
2 tablespoons chopped parsley
1 tablespoon snipped fresh chives
2 teaspoons chopped fresh tarragon or ½ teaspoon dried, crumbled
Freshly ground pepper
Salt

Pat shrimp dry. Heat oil in heavy large skillet over medium-high heat. Add shrimp and sauté until just opaque, about 3 minutes. Remove with slotted spoon and drain thoroughly on paper towels.

Remove all but 1 tablespoon oil from skillet. Place over medium-low heat, add garlic and stir 30 seconds. Pour in wine, increase heat and reduce mixture by ⅓. Add lemon juice and return to boil. Remove from heat. Swirl in butter 1 piece at a time, blending until creamy. Stir in parsley, chives and tarragon. Season with pepper. Taste and season with salt and additional lemon juice if desired. Arrange shrimp on individual plates. Spoon sauce over top and serve.

Coriander Shrimp Sauté

Serve this with steamed rice.

4 servings

¼ cup (½ stick) butter
16 uncooked large shrimp, peeled and deveined
1½ teaspoons coriander seeds, crushed

Salt and freshly ground pepper
¼ cup dry white wine
Fresh parsley sprigs

Melt butter in heavy large skillet over medium heat. Add shrimp, coriander, salt and pepper and stir until shrimp are just opaque, about 2 minutes. Add wine. Increase heat to high and boil 1 minute. Transfer to platter. Garnish with parsley and serve.

Shrimp Caborca

4 to 6 servings

½ cup (1 stick) butter
4 medium garlic cloves, crushed
2 to 3 large mild green Mexican chilies, coarsely diced or one 4-ounce can chopped green chilies
2 pounds medium shrimp,* shelled and deveined (tails removed)

Salt and freshly ground pepper
¼ cup fresh lime juice (about 2 medium limes)
¼ cup tequila
2 tablespoons chopped fresh parsley
Lime wedges (garnish)

Combine butter and garlic in large skillet over high heat and sauté garlic as butter is melting. When butter sizzles, discard garlic. Add chilies to skillet and cook just until butter begins to brown, about 1 minute. Add shrimp, salt and pepper. Sprinkle shrimp with lime juice and cook just until shrimp begin to color, stirring occasionally, about 2 to 3 minutes. Pour tequila into corner of pan; heat briefly and ignite, shaking pan gently until flame subsides. Remove from heat. Add parsley and toss to combine. Serve immediately with lime wedges.

*Large shrimp can be substituted. After shelling and deveining, butterfly shrimp to facilitate quick cooking.

Fireworks Shrimp

8 servings

2 tablespoons dried red pepper flakes
2 tablespoons red wine vinegar

1 cup tomato puree
10 tablespoons dry Sherry
6 tablespoons oyster sauce*
¼ cup soy sauce
2 tablespoons red wine vinegar
2 tablespoons sesame oil

1 tablespoon sugar
1 tablespoon grated fresh ginger
¼ cup clarified butter
¼ cup vegetable oil
48 large shrimp, peeled and deveined
1 pound cabbage, shredded
1 pound snow peas, trimmed
8 garlic cloves, minced
Freshly cooked rice

Soak dried red pepper flakes in wine vinegar in small bowl for 30 minutes.
    Blend next 8 ingredients. Set sauce aside.
    Heat butter and oil in heavy large skillet over medium-high heat. Add undrained red pepper flakes, shrimp, cabbage, snow peas and garlic and stir-fry until shrimp turn pink. Add sauce and cook until heated through. Serve hot over rice.

*Available at oriental markets.

Shrimp in Spicy Orange Sauce

8 servings

8 large oranges

3 tablespoons vegetable oil
1 teaspoon minced garlic
32 large uncooked shrimp, peeled and deveined
2 tablespoons Thai hot sauce* or hot pepper sauce

1 tablespoon firmly packed light brown sugar
1 tablespoon Worcestershire sauce
1 tablespoon cornstarch dissolved in 1 tablespoon cold water

Slice tops off oranges and discard. Scrape out pulp from shells; squeeze into bowl, reserving juice. Discard pulp. Set shells aside.

Heat oil in wok or heavy large skillet over medium-high heat. Add garlic and cook 1 minute. Add shrimp and stir-fry until opaque and bright pink, about 1 minute. Stir in hot sauce, brown sugar and Worcestershire. Add orange juice and bring to boil. Cook 2 minutes to blend flavors. Stir in dissolved cornstarch and continue cooking until sauce thickens, 2 to 3 minutes. Divide mixture among orange shells and serve.

*Available at oriental markets.

Shrimp in Green Sauce

2 servings

1 pound tomatillos,* husked
1 tablespoon minced Anaheim chili
1 tablespoon minced yellow guero chili
2 teaspoons minced jalapeño chili
1 teaspoon ground cumin
½ teaspoon salt
¼ teaspoon ground oregano
　Pinch of sugar

1 teaspoon vegetable oil
½ cup diced onion
1 garlic clove, minced

12 ounces uncooked shrimp, peeled and deveined
6 ounces zucchini, sliced ¼ inch thick
1 ounce sunchoke (Jerusalem artichoke),** peeled and sliced ¼ inch thick
½ cup chopped cilantro

Pierce each tomatillo in 2 places. Simmer until soft, about 12 minutes. Drain. Puree in processor. Strain tomatillos into bowl to eliminate seeds. Stir in chilies, cumin, salt, oregano and sugar.

Heat oil in heavy medium saucepan over medium-low heat. Add onion and garlic and cook until onion is translucent, stirring occasionally, about 10 minutes. Stir in tomatillo mixture. Cover and simmer until slightly thickened, about 15 minutes.

Add shrimp, zucchini and sunchoke to sauce and simmer until shrimp turn pink, about 5 minutes. Spoon onto platter. Garnish with chopped cilantro and serve.

*A vegetable that resembles a small green tomato. Available at most supermarkets.
**Keep in acidulated water until ready to use to prevent browning.

Gingered Shrimp with Asparagus and Green Onions

4 servings

1 pound large shrimp, shelled and deveined
2 large green onions, minced
3 tablespoons soy sauce
2 tablespoons mirin* (syrupy rice wine)
1 tablespoon oriental sesame oil
1 tablespoon minced fresh ginger
1 medium garlic clove, minced
½ teaspoon hot chili oil*
½ teaspoon finely grated orange peel
¼ teaspoon finely grated lemon peel

¾ cup chicken broth
2 tablespoons dry Sherry or Port
1 teaspoon cornstarch
　Nonstick vegetable oil spray
1 tablespoon oriental sesame oil
1½ pounds asparagus, trimmed, peeled and cut into 2-inch pieces
2 green onions, cut into matchstick julienne
1½ cups long-grain rice, cooked
　Orange peel julienne

Mix first 10 ingredients in medium bowl. Cover tightly and refrigerate 2 to 3 hours, turning occasionally.

Mix ½ cup broth, Sherry and cornstarch in small bowl. Coat heavy large skillet generously with vegetable spray. Add 1 tablespoon sesame oil and heat over high heat. Add shrimp with marinade and stir-fry until shrimp just turn pink, about 2 minutes. Transfer shrimp to bowl using slotted spoon. Add asparagus and remaining ¼ cup broth to skillet. Reduce heat to medium-low. Cover and cook until asparagus are crisp-tender, about 5 minutes. Stir cornstarch mixture and add to skillet. Return shrimp to skillet and stir until sauce turns translucent, about 2 minutes. Mix in green onion julienne. Mound rice in deep platter. Ladle shrimp mixture over. Garnish with orange peel julienne and serve immediately.

*Available at oriental markets.

Shrimp with Fresh Chives

2 servings

Melted butter
Coarse salt
Freshly ground white pepper
24 medium shrimp (about ½ pound), shelled and deveined (reserve shells)

Sauce
Reserved shells from shrimp
1⅓ cups chicken stock
⅓ cup dry white wine
2 tablespoons chopped shallot
2 tablespoons chopped carrot
2 parsley sprigs
1 garlic clove, lightly crushed

1 cup whipping cream

1 tablespoon unsalted butter
1¼ teaspoons fresh lemon juice
½ teaspoon coarse salt
Freshly ground white pepper
Pinch of ground red pepper
2 tablespoons chopped fresh chives

Preheat oven to 450°F. Lightly brush 4 ovenproof plates with melted butter and sprinkle lightly with salt and white pepper. Arrange 6 shrimp pinwheel fashion on each plate. Sprinkle with salt and pepper. Press small piece of buttered waxed paper on top of shrimp. Set plates aside.

For sauce: Combine shrimp shells, chicken stock, wine, shallot, carrot, parsley and garlic in medium saucepan. Cook over medium-low heat until liquid is reduced to about ¾ cup.

Heat cream in small saucepan.

Transfer shrimp shell mixture to processor and mix 30 seconds. Sieve through fine strainer into another pan, pressing to extract as much liquid as possible from shells and vegetables. Set pan over medium heat and slowly stir in heated cream. Bring to boil, reduce heat and simmer slowly until sauce is thickened and reduced to about 1 cup. Remove from heat and beat in butter. Season with lemon juice, salt, white and red pepper. Stir in chives.

Bake shrimp 4 minutes. Remove plates from oven, discard waxed paper and let plates stand for 40 seconds. Pour sauce over each portion and serve immediately.

Wild Rice and Shrimp Casserole

Use the microwave to prepare this delicious entrée.

4 to 6 servings

1 6-ounce package wild and long-grain rice mix

2 tablespoons (¼ stick) butter
1 cup sour cream
1 cup milk
2 tablespoons all purpose flour

½ cup thinly sliced onion
½ cup sliced mushrooms

¼ cup thinly sliced green bell pepper
¼ cup (½ stick) butter
1 tablespoon Worcestershire sauce
½ teaspoon freshly ground pepper
¾ pound cooked small shrimp

Cook rice in microwave or conventionally according to package directions.

Meanwhile, melt 2 tablespoons butter in 1-quart glass bowl on High for 30 to 40 seconds. Stir in sour cream, milk and flour, blending thoroughly. Cook on High, stirring frequently, until slightly thickened, about 3 to 4 minutes. Set aside.

Combine onion, mushrooms, green pepper and remaining butter in 2-quart glass baking dish. Cover and cook on High until vegetables are tender, about 4 minutes. Stir in rice, Worcestershire and pepper. Fold in cream sauce. Cover and cook on Medium (50 percent power) 15 minutes, turning dish halfway through cooking time. Stir in shrimp and serve hot.

Tarragon Shrimp Fettuccine

4 to 6 servings

½ cup (1 stick) butter
2 pounds medium shrimp, peeled and deveined
4 medium garlic cloves, minced
1 teaspoon dried tarragon, crumbled

2 cups whipping cream
1½ cups freshly grated Parmesan cheese

Pinch of cayenne pepper
2 tablespoons dry white wine
1 pound fettuccine, freshly cooked
3 tablespoons minced fresh parsley

Melt butter in large skillet over medium heat. Add shrimp, garlic and tarragon and stir until opaque and just pink, 1 minute. Remove using slotted spoon; set aside.

Add cream, cheese and cayenne to skillet and stir until bubbly, about 2 minutes. Mix in wine. Return shrimp to skillet. Toss gently until heated through, about 1 minute. Pour shrimp mixture over pasta. Toss to mix well. Sprinkle with parsley.

Bay Scallops with Lemon and Dill

4 servings

Nonstick vegetable oil spray
2 tablespoons (¼ stick) unsalted butter
1½ pounds bay scallops
⅔ cup dry vermouth

1 tablespoon fresh lemon juice
½ teaspoon finely grated lemon peel
¼ cup chopped fresh dill or ½ teaspoon dried dillweed
¼ teaspoon freshly ground pepper

Coat heavy large skillet generously with vegetable spray. Add butter and melt over medium heat. Add scallops and stir until almost opaque, about 2 minutes. Transfer to bowl using slotted spoon. Add vermouth, lemon juice and lemon peel to skillet and boil until reduced to thick glaze, about 5 minutes. Add any juices exuded by scallops and boil until reduced to glaze. Return scallops to skillet and stir until coated with sauce. Mix in dill and pepper. Serve immediately.

Sherried Scallops

4 servings

2 to 3 tablespoons butter
2 garlic cloves, minced
Pinch of fresh or dried tarragon
Pinch of fresh or dried oregano
1 pound sea scallops, cut into 1-inch pieces

Pinch of paprika
Salt and freshly ground pepper
Juice of ½ lemon
2 tablespoons Sherry
Fresh parsley sprigs and lemon slices (garnish)

Melt butter in large skillet over medium heat. Stir in garlic, tarragon and oregano. Add scallops and season with paprika, salt and pepper. Squeeze lemon juice over scallops and sauté until scallops turn opaque, about 4 to 5 minutes. Taste and adjust seasoning. Increase heat to high and add Sherry. Continue cooking, stirring constantly, until liquid has almost evaporated. Transfer scallops to shallow dish. Sprinkle additional paprika over top and garnish with parsley and lemon slices. Serve hot.

Scallops Chesapeake

4 servings

2 tablespoons (¼ stick) butter
8 ounces sliced mushrooms
2 teaspoons chopped fresh chives
Pinch of salt
Pinch of freshly ground pepper

1 pound fresh sea scallops, sliced into ¼-inch discs

½ cup whipping cream
¼ cup brandy

Melt butter in large skillet over high heat. Add mushrooms and sauté until tender, about 2 minutes. Sprinkle with chives, salt and pepper. Add scallops and sauté just until opaque, 2 to 3 minutes. Transfer scallops and mushrooms to 4 large scallop shells or ramekins using slotted spoon; keep warm.

Boil pan juices until reduced by half. Add cream and boil until reduced by half, stirring constantly. Heat brandy in small saucepan and ignite, shaking pan until flames subside. Blend brandy into sauce. Spoon over scallop mixture and serve.

Sea Scallops with Red Pepper Cream

6 servings

2 tablespoons (¼ stick) unsalted butter
2½ pounds sea scallops
Salt and freshly ground pepper

1 cup dry white wine
¼ cup medium-dry Sherry
1 cup whipping cream
½ cup Red Pepper Puree*

Heat butter in heavy large skillet over high heat. Add scallops, salt and pepper and stir until just opaque, 3 to 4 minutes. Transfer scallops to bowl, using slotted spoon. Add wine and Sherry to skillet and boil until reduced to syrup, stirring frequently, about 7 minutes. Whisk in cream and any juices in scallop bowl. Boil until thickened to sauce-like consistency, stirring occasionally. Whisk in Red Pepper Puree and heat through. Stir in scallops. Adjust seasoning. Serve immediately.

*Red Pepper Puree

Makes about 1 cup

¼ cup (½ stick) unsalted butter
2 pounds red bell peppers, diced
2 tablespoons sugar
2 tablespoons cider vinegar

1 teaspoon Hungarian sweet paprika
½ teaspoon dried red pepper flakes
Pinch of salt

Melt butter in heavy small saucepan over low heat. Stir in all remaining ingredients. Cover and cook until peppers are very soft, stirring occasionally, about 50 minutes. Uncover pan, increase heat to medium and stir until all liquid evaporates and peppers just begin to brown, about 10 minutes. Puree peppers through medium blade of food mill, discarding skins. *(Can be stored in refrigerator 1 week, or frozen.)*

Coquilles Saint-Jacques with Zucchini Mousse

2 servings

10 large sea scallops (about 12 ounces)
Melted butter
Coarse salt
Freshly ground white pepper

Zucchini Mousse

2 quarts (8 cups) water
2 tablespoons coarse salt
1 pound zucchini, thinly sliced

4 tablespoons (½ stick) unsalted butter, room temperature, cut into pieces

Vegetable Garnish
¼ cup julienne of leeks (white part only)
¼ cup julienne of carrots
¼ cup julienne of zucchini

2¼ teaspoons fresh lemon juice
1½ tablespoons water
¾ teaspoon coarse salt
Freshly ground white pepper

Cut scallops in half crosswise. Lightly brush 2 ovenproof plates with melted butter and sprinkle lightly with salt and pepper. Arrange 10 scallop slices in center of each plate. Sprinkle with salt and pepper. Press buttered waxed paper onto scallops.

For mousse: Bring 2 quarts water to boil in large saucepan with 2 tablespoons salt. Add sliced zucchini and cook uncovered 3 minutes. Drain immediately in colander and let stand 20 minutes, shaking occasionally to remove excess moisture.

Transfer zucchini to processor and puree until smooth, stopping machine several times to scrape down sides of bowl. Turn into nonaluminum saucepan and bring to boil over medium heat, stirring constantly. Remove from heat and whisk in butter one piece at a time until mousse is smooth and all butter is incorporated. Set saucepan over hot water to keep warm.

Preheat oven to 450°F.

For garnish: Bring another saucepan of salted water to boil. Combine leek and carrot in strainer and lower into boiling water for 30 seconds. Add zucchini and continue cooking 30 seconds. Remove strainer and let drain on paper towel, retaining water at boil.

Bake scallops 4 minutes. Meanwhile, stir lemon juice, water, remaining ¾ teaspoon salt and white pepper into mousse. Lower vegetables back into boiling water for 10 seconds to reheat.

Remove plates from oven and discard waxed paper. Spoon mousse around each serving of scallops. Garnish with vegetable julienne.

Scallops and Mussels in Dijon Mustard Vinaigrette

This elegant dish makes a perfect light luncheon entrée.

4 servings

20 bay scallops
⅔ cup fresh lemon juice
20 fresh mussels, cooked and shucked
  Dijon Mustard Vinaigrette*
  Boston lettuce leaves

2 ripe bartlett pears, peeled, cored and halved
  Avocado wedges or steamed asparagus spears (optional)
  Chopped fresh parsley

Marinate scallops in lemon juice 1 hour, stirring and turning several times. Discard lemon juice. Mix scallops, mussels and vinaigrette in small bowl. Line plates with lettuce. Set pears on lettuce. Top with avocado or asparagus, if desired. Arrange scallop mixture over. Sprinkle with parsley.

*Dijon Mustard Vinaigrette

Makes about 2 cups

1 medium hard-cooked egg, chopped
1 medium egg yolk
3 tablespoons Dijon mustard
1 tablespoon minced onion
2 teaspoons minced shallot
2 teaspoons chopped fresh oregano
2 teaspoons (or more) chopped fresh parsley

1 garlic clove, minced
1 teaspoon chopped fresh basil
½ teaspoon salt
  Pinch of sugar
  Freshly ground pepper
3 tablespoons white wine
3 tablespoons white wine vinegar
1 cup olive oil

Combine all ingredients except wine, vinegar and oil in medium bowl. Beat in wine and vinegar. Whisk in oil in slow steady stream. Cover vinaigrette and refrigerate until ready to use.

Steamed Clams and Mussels with Italian Sausage

2 servings; can be doubled or tripled

1 large tomato, seeded and chopped
4 teaspoons thinly sliced fresh basil
1 tablespoon thinly sliced fresh oregano
1 teaspoon olive oil
¾ pound hot Italian sausages
1 large leek (white part only), halved and thinly sliced
¼ teaspoon dried red pepper flakes

1 8-ounce bottle clam juice
½ cup dry white wine
1 tablespoon tomato paste
1 tablespoon Pernod
1 strip orange peel
  Freshly ground pepper
1½ pounds clams, scrubbed
¾ pound mussels, scrubbed and debearded

Combine tomato, basil and oregano in small bowl. Heat oil in heavy large saucepan over medium heat. Add sausages and sauté until brown and cooked through, about 10 minutes. Transfer to paper towels, using tongs or slotted spoon. Pour off all but 1½ tablespoons fat from pan. Add leek to pan and cook until tender, stirring frequently, about 10 minutes. Add pepper flakes and stir 30 seconds. Blend in clam juice, wine, tomato paste, Pernod and orange peel. Increase heat and bring to boil. Season with freshly ground pepper. Place clams in mixture. Cover and steam 3 minutes. Add mussels to saucepan. Cover and steam until shells open, shaking saucepan occasionally, about 5 minutes.

Cut sausages into ½-inch-thick pieces. Transfer shellfish to large bowl. Top with sausages and tomatoes.

Squid-Tomato Sauté

6 to 8 servings

2 tablespoons olive oil
3 garlic cloves, finely minced
1 28-ounce can Italian plum tomatoes, drained and coarsely chopped
⅓ cup dry white wine

6 small mushrooms, thinly sliced
4 green onions, thinly sliced
½ teaspoon dried basil, crumbled
Salt and freshly ground pepper
3 pounds squid, cleaned, sliced lengthwise into ¼-inch-wide strips

Heat oil in heavy large skillet over medium heat. Add garlic and sauté until soft and golden, about 2 minutes. Stir in tomatoes, wine, mushrooms, green onions and basil. Season with salt and pepper. Cook until heated through, about 5 minutes. Add squid and stir until opaque, 2 minutes.

🍎 *Index*

African, Peanut Butter Chicken, 86
Apple Sauerkraut Roast, 52
Asparagus
    Almonds and Mushrooms,
      Spaghetti with, 20
    Beef Paillards with, and Red Wine
      Sauce, 44
    Goat Cheese and Prosciutto,
      Creamy Scrambled Eggs with, 32
    and Green Onions, Gingered Shrimp
      with, 108
Autumn Soup, 2

Bacon-Cheese Oven Omelet, 33
Barbecued Chicken Wings and
    Spareribs, 85
Barbecued-hickory Shrimp, 105
Basil Tomato Sauce, 58
Basque Burgers (Lamb), 64
Bay Scallops. *See* Scallops
Beef, 42-56
    Bourbon Sandwiches, 16
    Burritos with Creamed Peppers, 42
    Carbonnade with Fresh Ginger, 54
    Chateaubriand, Garlic-roasted with
      Cognac-Mustard Sauce, 51
    Chateaubriand, Savory, 50
    Chili, Dynamite, 55
    Corned Brisket, Mustard-glazed, 52
    Curried, and Pasta Salad with
      Chutney Dressing, 14
    Flank Steak. *See* Flank Steak
    Hangover Hash, 55
    Marinated Sesame, 44
    Meat Loaf, Harvest, 56
    Mixed Grill Couscous, One-hour,
      42
    New York Strip Roast, Paniolo, 46
    and Olive Stew, 54
    Orange, with Snow Peas and Water
      Chestnuts, 43
    Paillards with Asparagus and Red
      Wine Sauce, 44

Paillards with Shiitake Mushrooms
    and Madeira, 45
Pepper Steak, 50
Pot Roast, Wine- and Herb-braised,
    51
Roast, Apple-Sauerkraut, 52
Short Ribs, Korean-style, 52
Steak Portuguese, 46
Steaks with Tarragon Butter, 46
Stroganoff, Burgundy, 53
Tamale Pie, Twenty-minute, 56
Tenderloin, Tournedos en
    Champagne, 50
and Vegetable Soup, Hearty, 4
and Vegetable Stew, Southwestern,
    53
Bell Pepper(s)
    Red, Broccoli and Chicken,
      Stir-fry of, 76
    Red, Puree, 112
    and Sausage, Italian, 72
    and Sausage Sandwich, 16
    Tricolored, Chicken Paillards with,
      84
    Turkey and Jicama Salad, 10
Bourbon Beef Sandwiches, 16
Brown Sauce, Quick, 45
Brunch. *See also* Cheese, Eggs
    Green Chili Quiche, 36
    Steeler's, 31
Burgundy Beef Stroganoff, 53
Burritos, Beef, with Peppers, 42

Cabbage, Napa, and Chicken Salad, 8
Cajun Shrimp, 106
Calf's Liver, Venetian Style, 56
Capellini with Zesty Crab Sauce, 22
Chateaubriand, Garlic-roasted with
    Cognac-Mustard Sauce, 51
Chateaubriand, Savory, 50
Cheese, 35-40
    Chèvre Cheesecake, 37
    Gruyère Torte, 37

Jalapeño Pie, 35
Pizza, Three-Cheese with Escarole
    and Garlic, 39
Potato-crusted Pizza, 40
Potato Soufflé, 37
Quiche, Chicken Liver and Bacon,
    36
Quiche, Green Chili, Brunch, 36
Roquefort Cheesecake, 38
Sausage Casserole, 35
Smoked Salmon Cheesecake, 38
Zucchini Casserole, Cheesy, 26
Cheesecake. *See* Cheese
Chicken, 76-91
    Baked with Tarragon Pesto, 88
    in Beer, 87
    and Cabbage Salad, 8
    Curry-glazed, 89
    German Style, Baked, 89
    Honey, Baked, 88
    Honey-Pecan Fried, 85
    Kapama, Baked, 89
    Liver, Bacon and Cheese Quiche, 36
    Livers with Apple, Carry's, 91
    Livers, Arroyo Perdido, 91
    Peanut Butter, 86
    and Pork Adobo, 87
    Roast with Garlic Croutons, 90
    Roast, Garlic and Rosemary, 90
    Salad Oriental, 10
    Salad with Pesto Dressing, 8
    Soup with Pimiento, Cream of, 5
    Stew with Fennel and Pernod, 87
    Stir-fry, Oriental, 76
    Szechwan Fried, 86
    Wings and Spareribs, Barbecued, 85
Chicken Breasts
    About Preparing, 49
    -Apple Sandwich, 15
    Baked Eggs with, in Tarragon Cream
      Sauce, 30
    with Balsamic Vinegar and Tomato-
      Pimiento Puree, 79

Broccoli and Red Bell Pepper, Stir-fry of, 76
Budapest with Homemade Noodles, 77
Chili with Yogurt and Avocado Topping, 77
with Chinese Mushrooms, 80
Cinnamon, 78
Curried with Green Cabbage and Red Apple, 84
with Irish Whiskey Sauce, 81
with Mustard Cream Sauce, 82
New Year's (Puffs), 90
Paillards with Spiced Tomato Sauce, 83
Paillards with Tricolored Bell Peppers, 84
Poached in Chèvre Cream Sauce, 81
Rinaldi with Mornay Sauce, 82
Rosato, 78
Scallops with Mustard Glaze, 83
Skewered Honey Lemon and Vegetables, 79
and Spinach Salad, 7
and Vegetable Julienne with Mustard-Walnut Vinaigrette, 9
Vineyard, 80
Chili
Chicken with Yogurt and Avocado Topping, 77
Dynamite, 55
Green, Brunch Quiche, 36
Vegetarian, 25
Chimichangas (Pork), 69
Chinese. See Oriental
Choucroute, Sausage, 73
Cinnamon Chicken, 78
Clam Chowder, New England-style, 7
Clams and Mussels, Steamed with Italian Sausage, 113
Confetti Pasta, 21
Coquilles Saint-Jacques with Zucchini Mousse, 112
Coriander Shrimp Sauté, 106
Corned Beef Brisket, Mustard-glazed, 52
Couscous, Mixed Grill, One-hour, 42
Crab
Curried, Garden Pea and Papaya Salad in Papaya Shells, 14
Omelet, Puffed, 34
Sauce, Zesty, Capellini with, 22
Curry(ied)
Beef and Pasta Salad with Chutney Dressing, 14
Chicken with Cabbage and Apple, 84
Crab, Garden Pea and Papaya Salad in Papaya Shells, 14
-glazed Chicken, 89
Lamb Shanks, 63
Turkey Salad, 11

Drunken Chops (Pork), 66
Dynamite Chili, 55

Eggplant
Lamb Tahini, 62
and Peppers, Pork Scallops with, Greek, 68
Stuffed with Almonds, Currants and Rice, 27
Eggs, 29-35
Baked with Chicken in Tarragon Cream Sauce, 30
Baked with Tomatoes and Kashkavàl Cheese, 30
Frittata, Hash, 35
Frittata, Mexican-style, 34
Mexicanos, 31
Omelet, Bacon-Cheese Oven, 33
Omelet, Crab, Puffed, 34
Poached with Tarragon Mushroom Sauce, 29
Scrambled, Chicken Livers Arroyo Perdido, 91
Scrambled, Creamy, with Asparagus, Goat Cheese and Prosciutto, 32
Scrambled, Creamy, Sautéed Veal Scallops with, 58
Scrambled, Creamy, with Smoked Turkey, Dill Butter and Peas, 32
Scrambled, Southwestern-style, with Shrimp and Corn, 33
Spinach Baked, 29
Steelers' Brunch, 31
Entertaining, Instant, About, 48-49

Fajitas, Rio Grande, 18
Fettuccine with Prosciutto, Rosemary and Peas, 21
Fettuccine, Tarragon Shrimp, 110
Fillet of Sole. See Sole
Fireworks Shrimp, 107
Fish, 94-103. See also Name of Fish
About Slicing, 48-49
Fillets Dijon, 94
Soup, de Poissons, 6
Stock, Simple, 104
Flank Steak
About Cutting, 49
Bacon-stuffed, 47
with Fresh Tomato Sauce, 48
Polynesian, 47
Florentine Lasagne Rolls with Shrimp Sauce, 24
Frittata, Hash, 35
Frittata, Mexican-style, 34
Fusilli with Zucchini, Plum Tomatoes, Basil and Parsley, 21

Garlic-roasted Chateaubriand with Cognac-Mustard Sauce, 51
Garlic-scented Mixed Vegetable Sauté with Pecans, 25
German Style Chicken, Baked, 89
Ginger Mayonnaise, 68
Gingered Shrimp with Asparagus and Green Onions, 108
Greek
Chicken Kapama, Baked, 89

Eggplant and Peppers, Pork Scallops with, 68
Lamb and Potato Stew, 65
Green Bean and Tuna Salad with Yogurt-Dill Dressing, 11
Green Chili. See Chili
Gruyère Torte, 37

Ham with Garlic Chili Sauce, 71
Ham Steak, Glazed, 72
Harvest Meat Loaf, 56
Hash Frittata, 35
Hash, Hangover, 55
Herb- and Garlic-marinated Leg of Lamb, 59

Indian Style Swordfish, 100
Instant Entertaining, About, 48-49
Irish Stew, Old-fashioned, 64
Irish Vegetable Stew, Braised, 4
Italian Sausage and Peppers, 72
Italian Sausage, Steamed Clams and Mussels with, 113

Jalapeño Cheese Pie, 35
Jambalaya, Seafood, 105

Kebabs. See Lamb Kebabs, Pork Kebabs
Kielbasa-Split Pea Soup, 5
Korean-style Short Ribs, 52

Lamb, 59-65
Chops, Grilled with Jalapeño Mint Sauce, 60
Chops Grilled with Thyme-Mustard Butter, 60
Chops Korabiak, 62
Chops Pan-fried with Cognac-Butter Sauce, 61
Chops Savory Sautéed, 61
with Eggplant Tahini, 62
Ground, Basque Burgers, 64
Hangover Hash, 55
Irish Stew, Old-fashioned, 64
Kebabs, Marinated, 60
Leg of, Herb- and Garlic-marinated, 59
and Lentil Salad with Curried Apple Vinaigrette, 15
Paillards with Tarragon and Garlic, 63
and Potato Stew, Greek, 65
Roast with Pine Nut and Parmesan Crust, 59
Shanks, Curried, 63
Lasagne Rolls Florentine with Shrimp Sauce, 24
Lasagne Rolls, Mushroom-stuffed, with Tomato Sauce, 23
Leek Tart with Cèpes, 28
Lemon Veal with Pink Peppercorns, 57
Lentil and Lamb Salad with Curried Apple Vinaigrette, 15
Liver. See Calf's Liver, Chicken Liver

Marinated
  Beef, Sesame, 44
  Chicken Wings and Spareribs,
    Barbecued, 85
  Lamb Kebabs, 60
  Leg of Lamb, Herb- and Garlic-, 59
  Swordfish, Lime, with Cilantro
    Butter, 101
Mayonnaise. *See also* Salad Dressing
  Curry, 11
  Ginger, 68
  Pesto, 95
  Tarragon, 13
Meat Loaf, Harvest, 56
Mexican
  Eggs Mexicanos, 31
  Shrimp Caborca, 107
  -style Frittata, 34
Microwave Dishes
  Chicken Rinaldi with Mornay
    Sauce, 82
  Italian Sausage and Peppers, 72
  Pasta with Walnut Sauce, 20
  Wild Rice and Shrimp Casserole, 110
Minestrone with Winter Pesto, 3
Mixed Grill Couscous, One-hour, 42
Mushroom(s)
  Asparagus and Almonds, Spaghetti
    with, 20
  Chinese, Chicken Breasts with, 80
  Sautéed, 47
  -stuffed Lasagne Rolls with Tomato
    Sauce, 23
Mussels and Clams, Steamed with
  Italian Sausage, 113
Mussels and Scallops in Dijon Mustard
  Vinaigrette, 113
Mustard-glazed Corned Beef, 52

New Year's Chicken (Puffs), 90
Noodles, Easy Homemade, Chicken
  Budapest with, 77

Omelet. *See* Eggs
Orange
  Beef with Snow Peas and Water
    Chestnuts, 43
  -glazed Pork Chops, 67
  Pork Kebabs, Aromatic, 66
Oriental
  Chicken Salad, 10
  Chicken Stir-fry, 76
  Shrimp and Vegetable Salad, 13
  Szechwan Fried Chicken, 86

Paniolo New York Strip Roast, 46
Papaya, Curried Crab and Garden Pea
  Salad in Papaya Shells, 14
Pasta, 20-24
  Capellini with Crab Sauce, 22
  Confetti, 21
  and Curried Beef Salad with
    Chutney Dressing, 14
  Fettuccine with Prosciutto,
    Rosemary and Peas, 21

Fettuccine, Tarragon Shrimp, 110
Fusilli with Zucchini, Plum
  Tomatoes, Basil and Parsley, 21
Lasagne Rolls Florentine with
  Shrimp Sauce, 24
Lasagne Rolls, Mushroom-stuffed,
  with Tomato Sauce, 23
Primavera, Rainbow, 20
with Scallops and Lemon Mustard
  Butter Sauce, 22
Spaghetti with Asparagus, Almonds
  and Mushrooms, 20
Tortellini in Bleu Cheese Sauce, 23
with Walnut Sauce, 20
Peanut Butter Chicken, 86
Pecan-crusted Pork Cutlets with
  Ginger Mayonnaise, 67
Pepper(s). *See also* Bell Pepper
  Creamed, Beef Burritos with, 42
  Steak, 50
Pesto
  Mayonnaise, 95
  Sauce, Winter, 3
  Spinach, 8
  Tarragon, Fresh, 88
Pie. *See also* Quiche, Tart, Torte
  Cheese, Jalapeño, 35
  Tamale, Twenty-minute, 56
Pizza
  Dough, Whole Wheat, 39
  Potato-crusted, 40
  Three-Cheese with Escarole and
    Garlic, 39
Polenta and Sausage Casserole, 73
Polynesian Flank Steak, 47
Pork, 65-71. *See also* Ham, Sausage
  and Chicken Adobo, 87
  Chimichangas, 69
  Chops with Beer and Ginger, 66
  Chops, Drunken, 66
  Chops Orange-glazed, 67
  Cutlets, Pecan-crusted with Ginger
    Mayonnaise, 67
  with Fennel, New Potatoes and
    Onion, 70
  Kebabs, Orange, Aromatic, 66
  Ribs with Sauerkraut, Country-
    style, 70
  Roast Loin of, in Lemon-Garlic
    Marinade, 65
  Scallops with Greek Eggplant and
    Peppers, 68
  Spareribs and Chicken Wings,
    Barbecued, 85
  Tenderloin with Peaches, 69
Portuguese Steak, 46
Pot Roast, Wine- and Herb-braised,
  51
Potato(es)
  Cheese Soufflé, 37
  -crusted Pizza, 40
  and Lamb Stew, Greek, 65
  Sole-stuffed, 96
Poultry. *See* Chicken, Turkey
Puree, Red Pepper, 112

Quesadillas, Open-face, 16
Quiche. *See also* Pie, Tart, Torte
  Cheese, Chicken Liver and Bacon,
    36
  Green Chili Brunch, 36

Red Snapper with Citrus, 97
Red Snapper Sautéed with Shallots and
  Pistachios, 97
Roast. *See* Beef, Lamb, Pork
Roquefort Cheesecake, 38
Rouille, 6

Salad, 7-15
  Beef, Curried, and Pasta with
    Chutney Dressing, 14
  Cabbage, Napa, and Chicken, 8
  Chicken Oriental, 10
  Chicken with Pesto Dressing, 8
  Chicken and Spinach, 7
  Chicken and Vegetable Julienne,
    Mustard-Walnut Vinaigrette, 9
  Crab, Curried, Garden Pea and
    Papaya in Papaya Shells, 14
  Dressing. *See also* Mayonnaise,
    Vinaigrette
  Dressing, Spinach Pesto, 8
  Lentil and Lamb with Curried Apple
    Vinaigrette, 15
  Salmon, Scotch, with Creamy Lime
    Dressing, 12
  Seafood Composée with Tarragon
    Mayonnaise, Summer, 12
  Shrimp and Vegetable, Oriental, 13
  Tuna and Green Bean with Yogurt-
    Dill Dressing, 11
  Turkey, Curried, 11
  Turkey, Jicama and Bell Pepper, 10
Salmon
  Grilled with Lime Cream Sauce, 98
  Sautéed with Spinach and Red Bell
    Pepper Sauce, 98
  Scotch, Salad with Creamy Lime
    Dressing, 12
  Smoked, Cheesecake, 38
  in Sorrel Sauce, 99
Salsa. *See also* Sauce
  Picante, 17
  Pico de Gallo, 18
Sandwich, 15-18
  Bourbon Beef, 16
  Chicken-Apple, 15
  Quesadillas, Open-face, 16
  Rio Grande Fajitas, 18
  Sausage and Bell Pepper, 16
  Tacos Grandes, Soft, 17
Sauce. *See also* Salsa
  Basil Tomato, 58
  Brown, Quick, 45
  Red Pepper Puree, 112
  Rouille, 6
  Shrimp, 24
  Tomato-Pimiento Puree, 79
  Verte, 2
  Winter Pesto, 3

Sauerkraut
Apple Roast, 52
Pork Ribs with, Country-style, 70
and Spareribs, Baked, 71
Sausage
and Bell Pepper Sandwich, 16
Cheese Casserole, 35
Choucroute, 73
Italian, Steamed Clams and Mussels
with, 113
and Peppers, Italian, 72
and Polenta Casserole, 73
Scallops
Bay, with Lemon and Dill, 110
Bay, Soup, 6
Chesapeake, 111
Coquilles Saint-Jacques with
Zucchini Mousse, 112
and Mussels in Dijon Mustard
Vinaigrette, 113
Pasta with, and Lemon Mustard
Butter Sauce, 22
Sea, with Red Pepper Cream, 111
Sherried, 111
Scrambled Eggs. See Eggs
Seafood. See also Fish, Name of
Seafood
Blanquette, Summer with Chard and
Snow Peas, 104
Composée Salade with Tarragon
Mayonnaise, Summer, 12
Jambalaya, 105
Shark
with Cilantro and Sour Cream
Sauce, 100
Mako, Piccata of, 99
Steaks in Oyster Sauce, 99
Shellfish, 104-14. See also Seafood
Short Ribs, Korean-style, 52
Shrimp
Caborca, 107
Cajun, 106
with Chives, Fresh, 109
and Corn, Southwestern-style
Scrambled Eggs with, 33
Fettuccine, Tarragon, 110
Fireworks, 107
Gingered, with Asparagus and Green
Onions, 108
in Green Sauce, 108
Hickory-barbecued, 105
Sauce, 24
Sauté, Coriander, 106
Sautéed with Garlic and Herbs, 106
Sole Fillet Stuffed with, 96
in Spicy Orange Sauce, 107
and Vegetable Salad, Oriental, 13
and Wild Rice Casserole, 110
Smoked Salmon Cheesecake, 38
Snapper. See Red Snapper
Sole
Fillet, Breaded, with Parsley-Lemon
Butter, 95

Fillet with Fresh Ginger, 94
Fillet Pesto, 95
Fillet Stuffed with Shrimp, 96
in Mustard Cream, 95
-stuffed Potatoes, 96
Soufflé, Potato Cheese, 37
Soup, 2-7
Autumn, 2
Beef and Vegetable, Hearty, 4
Chicken Pimiento, Cream of, 5
Clam Chowder, New England-style,
7
Fish Stock, Simple, 104
Kielbasa-Split Pea, 5
Minestrone with Pesto Sauce, 3
Poissons (Fish), 6
Rouille for, 6
Scallop, Bay, 6
Vegetable Stew, Braised Irish, 4
Southwestern Beef and Vegetable Stew,
53
Southwestern-style Scrambled Eggs
with Shrimp and Corn, 33
Spaghetti with Asparagus, Almonds
and Mushrooms, 20
Spareribs and Chicken Wings,
Barbecued, 85
Spareribs and Sauerkraut, Baked,
71
Spinach
Baked Eggs, 29
and Chicken Salad, 7
Florentine Lasagne Rolls with
Shrimp Sauce, 24
Pesto, 8
Salmon Sautéed with, and Red Bell
Pepper Sauce, 98
Split Pea-Kielbasa Soup, 5
Squash, Spaghetti, with Olive,
Anchovy and Caper Sauce, 26
Squid-Tomato Sauté, 114
Steak(s). See also Flank Steak
Pepper, 50
Portuguese, 46
with Zesty Tarragon Butter, 46
Steeler's Brunch, 31
Stew
Beef Carbonnade with Ginger, 54
Beef and Olive, 54
Chicken with Fennel and Pernod,
87
Chicken and Pork Adobo, 87
Irish, Old-fashioned, 64
Southwestern Beef and Vegetable,
53
Vegetable, Braised Irish, 4
Stir-fry of Chicken, Broccoli and Red
Bell Pepper, 76
Stir-fry, Oriental Chicken, 76
Stock, Fish, Simple, 104
Sukiyaki Swordfish, 101
Swordfish
with Ginger, Leek and Garlic, 102

with Grapefruit and Rosemary
Butter Sauce, 102
Indian Style, 100
Lime-marinated with Cilantro
Butter, 101
Sukiyaki, 101
Szechwan Fried Chicken, 86

Tacos Grandes, Soft, 17
Tamale Pie, Twenty-minute, 56
Tart. See also Pie, Quiche, Torte
Leek with Cèpes, 28
Tomato
Basil Sauce, 58
-Pimiento Puree, 79
-Squid Sauté, 114
Torte, Gruyère, 37
Tortellini in Bleu Cheese Sauce, 23
Tournedos en Champagne, 50
Trout with Shrimp, Chives and Cream,
103
Trout, Spiced Pan-fried, 102
Tuna and Green Bean Salad with
Yogurt-Dill Dressing, 11
Turkey
Hash with Sweet Potatoes and
Turnips, 92
Jicama and Bell Pepper Salad, 10
Paillards with Capers, Crisp, 92
Salad, Curried, 11

Veal, 57-58
About Preparing, 49
Lemon with Pink Peppercorns, 57
Paillards with Chive Cream, 57
Sautéed, with Scrambled Eggs, 58
Vegetable, 25-28. See also Name of
Vegetable
and Beef Soup, Hearty, 4
and Beef Stew, Southwestern, 53
and Chicken Julienne with Mustard-
Walnut Vinaigrette, 9
and Chicken, Skewered Honey
Lemon, 79
Cutlets, Spicy, 26
Sauté, Mixed, Garlic-scented with
Pecans, 25
and Shrimp Salad, Oriental, 13
Soup, Autumn, 2
Soup, Minestrone with Winter
Pesto Sauce, 3
Stew, Irish, Braised, 4
Vegetarian Chili, 25
Vinaigrette, Dijon Mustard, 113
Vineyard Chicken, 80

Whole Wheat Pizza Dough, 39
Wild Rice and Shrimp Casserole, 110
Wine- and Herb-braised Pot Roast, 51

Zucchini Casserole, Cheesy, 26
Zucchini and Plum Tomatoes, Fusilli
with, 21

 # Credits and Acknowledgments

The following people contributed the recipes included in this book:

Jean Anderson
Demetra Andronico
Christine Baumhefner
Jeffree Brooks
Sue Cam
Diana Cavey
Ginger Chang
Rebecca Chase
Jo Colter
Evelyn Cunha
Sandre Cunha
John Cusimano
Maggi Dahlgren
Anita and Paul DeDomenico
Claudia Ebeling
Sue Ellison
Carol Field
Catherine Firestone
Nancy Friedlander
Peter Gaillard
Dorothy Garrison
Kay Garrity
Judith Gerstein
Peggy Glass
Sandra Gluck
Matty Goldberg
Deirdre Luchsinger-Goldberg
Bunny and Sidney Goldman
Marion Gorman
Grand Central Oyster Bar, New York, New York
Freddi Greenberg
David Griffin
Connie Grigsby
Gritti Palace, Venice, Italy
Carol Haggett
Barbara Hansen
Gloria Harris
John Hartman
Mark Hawthorne

Hemingway's, Sonora, California
Sandy Hoffman
Doreen Howard
Maria Jacketti
Nehama Jacobs
Earl T. Johnson
Rhonda Jones
Jane Helsel Joseph
Linda Kamerman
Barbara Karoff
Lynne Kasper
Karen Kaplan
Kristine Kidd
Greta Kinderman
Kay Koch
Maureen Kolis
Kristina Korabiak
Heidi Landers
Lynne Lang
Le Club, Ketchum, Idaho
Faye Levy
Susan Loomis
Ivan and Nan Lyons
Robert Magretta
Abby Mandel
Copeland Marks
Sunny Marx
Robert McClellan
Rae McIntee
Michael McLaughlin
Carmela Meely
Alyce Faye Morgan
Jefferson and Jinx Morgan
Judy Murray
David Nover
Katie Nunes
Beatrice Ojakangas
Helen Cassidy Page
Cindy Pawlcyn
Robin Peek

Sharon Perlman
Sara Perry
Pirates' House Restaurant, Savannah, Georgia
Thelma Pressman
The Quechee Inn, Quechee, Vermont
Ruedell Reaves
Elizabeth Reily
Sandy Ringel
Phyllis Rizzi
Carol Robertson
Joan Robinson
Betty Rosbottom
Dorothea Sagal
Bess Samaras
Linda Sansot
Richard Sax
Rita Schlansky
Schroeder's Cafe, San Francisco, California
Susan Seitz
Andrea Shapiro
Joan Shaw
Morgan Sheriden
Siamese Princess, Los Angeles, California
Terry Thompson
Jane Trittipo
Dorothy Vusich
Jere Wade
Charlotte Walker
Jane Wallace
Tonee Wilen
Janie Wilson
Isabel Wood
Linda Wray
Yianni's Restaurant, Claremont, California

Additional text was supplied by:
Jane Helsel Joseph, *Instant Entertaining*.

Special thanks to:

Editorial Staff:
Angeline Vogl
MaryJane Bescoby

Graphics Staff:
Bernard Rotondo
Gloriane Harris

Rights and Permissions:
Karen Legier

Indexer:
Rose Grant

The Knapp Press
is a wholly owned subsidiary of
KNAPP COMMUNICATIONS CORPORATION

Composition by PTH Typographers, Los Angeles, California

This book is set in Sabon, a face designed by Jan Teischold in 1967 and based on early fonts engraved by Garamond and Granjon.